SOMETHING ABOUT ILION

An Interpretation of Homer's Epic Poem, the Iliad
Translated from Greek and Latin extants and
readings from Fitzgerald
Books I - V

By Zaldy C. De Leon Jr.

POETRY PLANET
Builder Of Dreams

PREFACE

There were already several translations of Homer's Iliad by great poets, renowned men of letters, and by them who dedicated their lives in the writings of the masters, both in poetic and prose editions. These classics were made available to us, and it seems that another one is no longer necessary. However, as a student of literature and history, there is a natural need to satisfy the intellect. There is some unquiet soul inside that really needs to express some creative endeavor. Like a flower inside a bud and a butterfly inside a cocoon. I cannot spend my years in solitary, I need to see the beauty of the world, it says to me. With it, I find inspiration with Homer – which I believe is truly one of the oldest, and the greatest works of creative writing and classical history.

Many people may find this impertinent or unnecessary, but I toil not to think of myself as someone whose endeavors are important, but still, as a student of the masters whose traditions of love for their craft exceeds the thoughts of what others may say. In acquired a copy of Robert Fitzgerald's 1974 Linear Translation from a used book store. This book becomes the foundation of my work. This work is based on that translation. Fitzgerald's edition is linear translation which is a line-by-line translation from the original text. I thought why not versify this translation into verse? I worked on with a quatrain in pentameter with 10-syllabes rhyme pattern. The original translation runs in a free verse or somewhat in an informal prosaic. But since I love lyrical poems, I tried to 'versify' these linear translation to verse. Take note that this is not a translation nor a transliteration but a versification of the linear translation. I do not know if another Filipino has tried his hands on Homer in this same manner as I did, but if there's not one student who made it, then this work is a representative of which, and Homer may be glad in it.   I do not intend this work to be published, so furnishing few copies of the work would do me happiness. I just want this work to be a part of some loving library where it would be kept and read by people who may find interest in it. May the Muses smile on me. Here, my dear Rizal.

Dinalupihan, Bataan
Summers, 2017

BRIEFING ON HOMER'S ILIAD

Introduction

Iliad, ancient Greek epic poem in 24 books attributed to the poet Homer. It was probably composed in the 8th century bc, but it describes events of the Trojan War, a conflict between Greece and Troy that took place four centuries earlier. The initial cause of the Trojan War was the abduction of Helen, the queen of Sparta, by Paris, a Trojan prince. The Iliad relates in 15,693 lines a momentous episode in the Trojan War—the wrath of the Greek hero Achilles and its destructive consequences.

The Action

The action of the Iliad begins in the tenth and final year of the Greek siege of Troy. The Greek army has been besieging Troy for over nine years. In a recent raid on a nearby district, the Greeks have captured Chryseis, daughter of a priest of the god Apollo. Agamemnon, commander in chief of the Greek forces, has taken her for his slave woman. Apollo in anger afflicts the Greeks with a devastating plague after Agamemnon humiliates the priest.

The Wrath of Achilles. At an assembly of the army Agamemnon, urged by Achilles, agrees to send back Chryseis. But he insists that he shall have Briseis, Achilles' captive, in her place. Achilles, in anger at this slight on his honor, draws his sword to attack

Agamemnon, but is restrained by the goddess Athena who wishes the Greeks to win the war. Achilles abuses Agamemnon as a shameless and selfish coward and announces his withdrawal from active service in the war.

Nestor, by far the oldest and wisest of the Greek kings, tries to reconcile the quarrelers, but fails. Chryseis is restored to her father by Odysseus, the most diplomatic and effective of the Greek commanders. Agamemnon takes Briseis, and Achilles asks his mother, Thetis, to persuade Zeus, the king of the gods, to allow the Trojans to win a victory, so that the Greeks may learn how much they owe to his valor and honor him accordingly. Zeus consents despite protests from his wife Hera, who favors the Greeks.

The Armies Prepare. Zeus sends a deceptive dream to Agamemnon, who calls a council of the commanders. Confusion follows: The army is seized by a sudden desire to return home, but Odysseus, prompted by Athena, checks the rush toward the ships with a powerful speech. Thersites, the only ugly and mean-spirited soldier in the poem, boldly insults Agamemnon until Odysseus stops him with abusive language and blows. After a prudent speech from Nestor and a sacrifice to the gods, the whole Greek army, except Achilles and his followers, prepares for battle.

A detailed description of the forces contributed by each Greek state (the so-called Catalogue of the Ships) follows. The use of colorful poetic descriptions saves it from being a dry list. The Trojan army assembles to resist the attack and is described in a briefer catalogue. The army is led by Hector, the chivalrous and valiant son of Priam, king of Troy. Hector's brother Paris has caused the war by abducting Helen, wife of Menelaus, king of the Greek state of Sparta.

The Battle Begins. Paris offers to fight a duel with Menelaus to settle the conflict. After an exchange of blows, Paris's protector, the goddess Aphrodite, intervenes to save him. Treacherously incited by their enemy Athena, the Trojans break the armistice made before the duel and thereby put themselves morally in the wrong. A series of single combats ensue, skillfully interspersed with domestic incidents inside Troy.

Eventually, when the Greeks are hard-pressed by the Trojans, Agamemnon sends representatives to Achilles who offer rich gifts and the return of Briseis if he will join the fight again. Achilles refuses because he knows reentry guarantees his death at Troy and he now believes no form of honor is worth his life. Yet, after the Greek warrior Ajax appeals to him as a friend, Achilles announces he will fight again if Hector reaches their ships.

The Death of Patroclus. Further duels and maneuvers follow. The Trojans attack the Greek camp, and Hector seems unstoppable. Hera, fearing a Trojan triumph, adorns and beautifies herself voluptuously and lures Zeus away from helping the

Trojans. He and she withdraw together to Mount Ida. The Greeks regain the upper hand. Zeus awakens, furiously realizes Hera's cunning, and gives help again to the Trojans. The Greeks fall back in panic. Pitying their plight, Patroclus, dearest friend of Achilles, puts on Achilles' armor and drives the enemy back. But Hector meets Patroclus in single combat and kills him, and a bloody battle rages over his corpse.

The Death of Hector and the Funeral of Patroclus. Achilles resolves to avenge his friend's death. Thetis persuades Hephaestus, god of metalworking, to make a beautiful new suit of armor for her son. The ornamentation of the shield is described in detail: It includes civic and rural scenes and dancing figures. Achilles, equipped with his new armor, sallies out and kills many Trojans. He fights the river-god Scamander and finally encounters Hector, who panics and is chased three times by Achilles around the walls of Troy. Achilles overtakes Hector and with the help of Athena kills him remorselessly. He ties Hector's corpse by the heels to his chariot and drags it exultantly back to the Greek camp, while Priam, Priam's wife Hecuba, and Andromache, Hector's devoted wife, bewail Hector's death.

Achilles makes preparations to give Patroclus a hero's funeral. A feast is given; wood is gathered from the forests of Mount Ida for a great pyre. Patroclus's corpse is laid on the pyre; the funeral rites are performed, the body is consumed by fire, and the bones are gathered in a golden vessel. Then come athletic contests in his honor.

The next day Achilles, still full of grief, drags the body of Hector round the burial place of Patroclus repeatedly. After twelve days Apollo appeals to the gods to end this indignity. Zeus agrees to allow Priam to ransom the body of his son, despite the opposition of Hera. Thetis is sent to persuade Achilles to consent to the return of Hector's body. Iris, messenger of the gods, tells Priam of Zeus's decision. Priam, despite Hecuba's efforts to dissuade him, sets out for the tent of Achilles, bearing rich gifts as a ransom.

In a somberly magnificent scene Achilles receives Priam with grave courtesy and, remembering his own aged father Peleus (whom he knows he will never see again), gives Priam the body of Hector. Priam returns with it to Troy. Andromache mourns her husband, Hecuba her son, and Helen her friend. The Trojans perform the obsequies of Hector, and the poem ends with the line: "So they tended the burial of Hector, tamer of horses."

The Characters

The characters of the Iliad are lifelike, vivid, and memorable. On the Greek side are the arrogant, self-centered, yet majestic Agamemnon and the young, quick-tempered, and honor-obsessed Achilles. Savage in his anger, Achilles at heart remains courteous and compassionate. Nestor, though prudent and subtle, is often long-winded. Odysseus, hero of the other epic attributed to Homer, is conciliatory, self-controlled, and resourceful; Ajax, bold, massive, and magnanimous; and Diomedes, dashing and debonair. Many others are portrayed with masterly variety and clarity.

Among the Trojans are the valiant, affectionate, lovable, and doomed Hector, and the age-worn, grief-stricken, but undefeated Priam. Hecuba, wild with grief, first tries in vain to coax her son back to safety, then laments his death in utterly hopeless grief. Andromache, noblest of young wives and mothers, appears in one of the most moving scenes ever composed: the final parting between her and Hector. Helen, conscious of the destructive element in her supreme beauty, remains helpless to escape it.

The gods, too, have vivid but by no means admirable personalities. They bicker, quarrel, scheme, deceive, and even come to blows; they provide the only moments of humor in the grim story. Yet Zeus is invested at times with a sublimity that approaches the highest conceptions of deity. There also are many glimpses of minor characters—soldiers, mythological figures, captives, servants, and country folk—in the background. No poet has surpassed Homer in the art of subtle, economical character drawing.

CONTENTS

Book I
THE DISAGREEMENT

O immortal one, let anger be sung,
Doomed and ruinous, Akhilleus' fang,
Causing the Akhaians a bitter loss,
Heaving souls their fall, down their brave heroes!

And their flesh upon depressed soil of tears,
In the undergloom of death disappears,
Leaving but memorials of death and blood,
Carrion for birds of prey and dogs in mud.

Let the will of Zeus be done, this time on,
Whilst heaven attests to the future throne.
When two brave souls contended against,
Broke each other's name their powerful raze,

Lord Agamemnon, Marshall of the Greeks,
And most arduous fright, called prince of the beasts.
The former, Atreus' son, lord and king,
The latter, Akhilleus, goddess bring!

To the gods of Olympus, I beseech,
Who brought this quarrel in a height bewitched?
That peace may not settle that easily,
But a brawl in which our contenders see.

Thus, the son of Zeus by Leto bespeak,
His anger unto Agamemnon's wick,
This man so rude his words and iron will,
To a god nonetheless might keep him still.

Therefore, the god made a great burning wind,
To consume the army, lessen it thin,
So the plague arise, and the army woed,
Sickened and dying in the whole abode,

The curse named for a single man has been
The army's plead to surrender his din,
From despising a man of prayer, flee,
Look how suffer they, this calamity?

This old priest, the man of prayer, Khryses,
In a ship comes down with gifts so priceless,
A mean to ransom his fair daughter back,
This he pursue to Agamemnon's mock,

Thus, on a golden staff he carried on,
The white bands of god, more than precious stone,
He plead for grace to all men Akhaian,
Chiefly to the two powers in the land!

Says Khryses, "O captains, honor I say,
Thou Menelaos, brother-master, pray,
And Agamemnon mighty-king, and all
Thou, Akhaian men, listen to my soul!

Olympus beholds the gods in that grace,
May they grant you plunder to Priam's place,
And that afterwards, a fair wind to home,
But give back my daughter for a ransom."

Then, all the soldiers murmured their assent:
"O Menelaos, Agamemnon, spend
No time to think of this good man's request,

As we too honored Apollo, arrow's best!

Thus, behave well to the priest, O great king,
Take the ransom, give his daughter you bring,
For see how this priest's blessing for us may,
In Priam's gallantry we shall but stay!"

But Agamemnon's rash would not comply,
It went against his desire, so he deny,
And brutally ordered the old priest out,
To the eyes of the gods such act's uncouth,

Says Agamemnon, "Let me not find you,
Anywhere by the waters or land, sue
Me unto your gods, but I won't comply,
I am Agamemnon, and you know why…

Return not, you old priest, never come back,
Forget your daughter in my hands a-luck,
And if I do, those effects can't help you,
The white bands of your gods will say adieu,

They will fail your heart until you die soon,
And see nay your daughter thus if you swoon,
Should I give her up? No, I will not do,
But she's mine forever, I swear to you.

She will grow old at my home in Argos,
Far away from her own country, or worse,
Works on my loom, and visiting my bed,
This shall be her fate as my will has said.

So leave us in peace and go, while you can,

Do not show your face again to me! Ran
Away! – if ever you found my shadow,
Do not come back and witness your sorrow."

So harsh he was, in a voice of terror,
The priest's knees shook, he gets out of the door,
That the old man feared, thus obeyed his word,
Moves away silently, dread by the lord.

But unto the shore, a clamorous sea,
He prayed and prayed to the gods, intensely,
As he cease from solemn, as he forego,
Silken-braided god, summons for Leto:

"O hear me, master of the silver bow,
Righteous protector of Tenedos, know
That your servant here pleads, render my woe!
Your holy towns summon you, Apollo!

O Sminthian, I have been loyal vast,
Roofed your temples and shrines, as do I must,
Golden cups and silver bowls in your name,
Bronze statues and iron swords, just the same.

Or burnt thighbones and fat in your altar,
These things I've done for your glory stellar!
For highly we venerate your strength wide,
Hear your humble servant, my soul unhide,

Bullock or goat flesh – let my wish come true,
An old man's heart has just one thing for you,
But your arrows on the Danaäns strike,
Recompense my tears, snare the way you like."

Hearing the priest's prayer from Olympus,
Phoibos Apollo, the bidded god roused,
With storm he walked in his heart at his best,
Angered by Agamemnon's interest!

With regal quiver and bow on his back,
And silver arrows in a bundle stacked,
The sky has clanged a mighty nimbus fright,
As he rocked every waters with his might!

His anger descending like brimming stone,
Darkness that flung like death itself enthroned,
The waters rolling high, the ships are threatened,
He halted not a wind against the den,

Where cruel Agamemnon needs to face,
As Apollo's bowstring condemned their place,
The silver bow sprang, thunders gone a craze,
Both men and beast beholds a god dismays.

Beast of the meadows and the forest woods,
Foxes and dogs were his target to wounds,
No innocent beast is counted to rule,
But first were they in this list from the whole,

For next target were men, mighty or not,
Army, farmer, Apollo's anger's hot!
Soon they felt the enthralling pain and irk,
They were sore afraid, none of them may lurk.

Skulk in the field for corns or oat meal spare,
Prowl in the vineyard for some grapes to lair,

Day and night, under the gloomy darkness,
The god's hard shots were pointed all unrest,

The pyres are burned all nine days from that time
When the first thunder greeted them sublime,
The army could have been decimated
But Agamemnon firmly raised his head!

On the tenth day, great Akhilleus stand
To call the army, as he understand
What these thunder may have been saying so,
How angry could that god name Apollo.

So rank and file, under treacherous clouds,
He assembled this still great remaining goads,
That Hera may took pity on his men,
She moved him to it, so that it may end.

Under the arms of great Hera the queen,
Those ivory arms of protection, win,
Unto dying Danaäns, her shield is strong,
For a meantime neglect the kingly wrong,

All being mustered, all place and quiet,
Then Akhilleus runs like a lion, said:
"Agamemnon, now, I take it, to you,
The siege is broken, we are off, adieu!

The sail is ready, our fate is all clear
We should have listened to priest Khryses clear,
We will sail and we'll not leave death behind,
Consider it right now, with sword and mind!

Consult a priest or some diviner now,
Even some fellow good at dreams endow'd,
Then, this fate, shall we embark in our heart,
Is time's proper history we'll impart.

Come down, O Zeus, king of the gods, as well,
Answer, why all this anger to us dwell
By that god Apollo? Is Khryses priest
To his oracles and great mysteries?

Has he some quarrel against our people,
In our vows or hekatombs or our wall?
Is a mutton not enough for his joy,
Do we need to sacrifice a young boy?

Or, smoking goat flesh makes him lift this plague?
When, even innocent people had ache
Over the pain of loss, o'er death and woe,
Spread over the land in winding throw?

Should a daughter be sacrifice to him,
And let her blood strew, as litanies teem?
I will let our priests sung prayers all year,
But why punish us, and cause children fear?"

After offering the question, he sat,
Down he sat in deep meditation, That
A Kalkhas Theorides, wisest man,
Wisest by far of all who understand

The flight of the birds in the upper sky,
Thus, he knew what was, what had been, today
And what the future may had, seem to be,

He went unto Akhilleus, pray thee.

Through the gift of Apollo divining,
Their ships went unto Illion, he bring,
Akhaia's men unto their holy words,
Concludes the journey and their bloody swords.

Kalkhas said: "O listen, Akhilleus,
Your countenance and name, so dear to Zeus!
It is on me you call to tell you why
The Archer God is angry though we cry.

Well, I can tell you, honestly and whole,
But if I dare to speak thus afterall,
You have to back me up, and defend me,
Against him whom I might enrage gravely,

For these men obey his words, as it is,
The man at Argos, powerful beast!
O Akhilleus, listen to me well,
Less you follow these words, then will I tell.

A great man in his rage formidable,
For mentioning his name 'gainst the fall,
Why these things happen against your silence,
Thunders that kill from great Apollo, hence,

The fire in his belly might be exposed,
And defenseless Kalkhas here be disposed,
So decide whether you will protect me,
Then shall I say the sole reason to thee."

Akhilleus said, "Courage, Kalkhas, come,

Tell what you know, I seek not a sham,
Give light to these things that matters to me,
And I shall swear Apollo to save thee.

O Apollo, the lord god whom you pray
When you uncover the truth in its sway,
Never while I draw breath, while I can see,
Shall any man in this beachhead dare thee

Lay hands on you --- not one of the army,
Not Agamemnon, if you meant is he,
For he's the powerful man at Argos!
But worry not, I tell you, in this cause

Though he is first in rank among these men,
Shall I protect you though my breath is bent,
I thought it well, Kalkhas, so come and say
The words I need to hear without delay."

The diviner took heart and said, "There is
Not a failure in hekatombs, no less
On your vows; neither on your piece of meat!
For none of these is held against our feat!

But of the man of prayer, him I knew,
Unto Agamemnon's contempt must drew,
Apollo thus summoned by him he bade,
Against that brutish man, the Archer laid.

The brutish man kept the priest's daughter fine,
Spurned his gifts, and threatened him unrefined.
So the priest pleads unto Apollo's grace,
And the result was this plague in our place!

Now, at this present, it might never cease
Until Agamemnon complied at ease,
But unwillingly, this master shall not
Cause to submit unto Apollo's tat.

Danaäns shall not be relieved on this,
His plague shall not be taken back dismissed,
Until that girl who turned the eyes of men
Be restored to her own father --- the end

Cannot be seen by now, as long as she
Was not delivered fairly and freely,
Without ransom to pay --- at his reside,
And offer up a hekatomb abide

There at Khryse where the old priest await,
Then, shall we calm Apollo's raging hate,
Offer up her daughter back, build him shrine,
Apollo shall listen in these define."
He finished and sat down. Then enraged by
This speech, the son of Atreus thus sigh'd,
The ruler of the great plain, in fury
Rose; anxious to daze down their enmity.

His heart swelled in annoyance huge, resent
Kalkhas' words with fuming chaos and grunt,
His eyes shone out like licking fire inflame,
Then, with a long boding look, he declaim:

"You visionary of hell, Kalkas, halt!
Never have I had fairplay 'gainst your tongue,

Should I not be angered by that forecast?
I am but a natural man, alas!

Hardship is all you care about, or see,
And no happy knowledge for this city!
And you bring nothing to pass but omen
That captures fear and horror to our men!

Your ides are pastures of death and dread,
Calling out all beasts their ruins ahead,
They grazed the hill for poisons you have thrown,
And finally, in gaiety wide, disowned.

Here you stand again before the army,
Giving it out as oracle weary
That the Archer made them suffer greatly
Because of the impudence within me?

Thus, from not taking the ransom gift,
And let Khryseis go, then plague he'll lift,
How prudent are your words against me, priest?
Your words are visions from the hellish mist!

Now, I tell you, I shall have her at home,
Do not dare ask me to take the ransom!
For, aye, if I took her unto my lair,
That's because she's more than worthy affair,

To my own wife Klytaimnestra, she rate
Higher that she'll be her own jealous fate,
She loses nothing by comparison
In mind or skill, in beauty or passion.

For all of that, I am willing to yield,
If it is the best, then let gods fulfilled,
I want the army be saved, not destroyed,
Cease from your words just then to me annoyed,

You must prepare however, boldly march,
A prize of honor for me, go forth, start!
That I may not be left without portion –
I, of all Argives – halt from this motion!

It is not fitting, I think, in this time,
While every man of you looks but sublime,
My girl goes elsewhere, I cannot her find,
Though circumstances say, I might be blind."

In this, with rampant jest, the warrior he,
Prince Akhilleus answered wise to thee:
"Lord Marshall, most insatiate of men,
How can the army make you gift attend?

Where is the store of booty? Can I see?
Everything plundered from the town has flee!
Gold and silver in every baskets gone,
In greed it vanish with all these your men.

Just let the girl go, as Kalkhas have sooth,
That we may gather our fields and our fruit!
Free that girl of yours, in thy god's name, now,
And this very plague upon us bestow

The peace we all wanted, twice over, three
Times over, just to attain the key

In which we would sack Troy in victory,
And crush down the ring of that stone city!"
Agamemnon answered, thus: "Not that way
Shall I answer your plead, not now, not today,
I will not be gulled by that strength you fire,
My word shall not be bent by your desire,

Akhilleus, if you want, take me in,
Or try to get behind me, if you win!
What do you really ask out of me, then?
But that I can't do whilst clamor I lend?

When you want your winnings, it is all yours,
But my own prize is mine, O from that hours!
Do you want me give her up, and sit here,
As if something's been taken, out of fear?

Oh no! The army will award a prize
To me and make sure my contentment wise,
For they knew me, in the most astute way,
And in the shrewdest spear to curse this day!

Or if they do not, the girl I'll take own,
Or Odysseus' prize, or Ajax, or your own?
Would you take her, to keep? I do not care,
But this, I tell you, I'll stick my affair,

In the deepest silence, or highest brawl,
In the longest days, or shortest control,
Into this throne that other gods may see,
It's Agamemnon who makes history!

Her father may choke of anger and tears

But I care not, Khryseis is my cheers!
Tell him, therefore thus, I will not be bent,
Agamemnon's word is a steel ahead.

Look to it now, look what have I done so,
We launch on the great sea, before you know,
The beauty that was war against your heart,
But a warrior never cease from his art!

Look again there! A well-found ship I manned
With oarsmen and sacrificial beasts, then
Put aboard Khryseis in her beauty
And loveliness. Therefore, my deputy,

Ajax, Idomeneus, or Odyseus,
Or even you, fearsome Akhilleus,
Will make a hekatomb from her at sea,
And quiet the Archer of his sultry."

Akhilleus frowned a mighty anger,
Looked at Agamemnon, say the bitter:
"You thick-skinned, shameless, greedy fool, I say,
Can any Akhaian in here obey?

Or have anyone care for you, pray thee,
After this on marches, or in the sea?
After the battle, which you'll laid your see?
Give these men and their swords some dignity!

I think nay – no one cares about your greed,
Therefore, why should they contribute your need?
As for myself, when I came here to fight,
Troy had no quarrel with me, just enlight,

I had no quarrel with Troy either, thus,
A Trojan spearman has no quarrel passed.
This, I say, to you, Agamemnon, hear:
They never stole a cattle from me drear.

No horses they get out of my old house,
Not a single basin of water they rouse.
They never try to get a rope and snatch,
No sword have they minted against my watch,

No Trojan priest has cursed my land and air,
Save me troubles in a frightening nightmare,
But greater I think, the more I see that
We never had any problems to splat!

Never in Phthia, in my land of birth,
Had their peace in us cut in obvious girth
When they had none to see, and none to own,
For they themselves had plenty in their throne!

Never in our black farm they ravaged crops,
Not a single wheat has been picked and dropped,
For how many miles are our lands between,
A wildering waters, an open sea…

Nay, we joined for you, you insolent fool,
Raise your name with our steels and swords awhole,
To fight for Menelaos, to please you,
And avenge his pride with my splendid crew.

But the Trojans are but clear against us
Your revenge is not worthy of our dust,

Second to my knowledge, the virgin lass,
To get her, nay, but over my carcass.

You flouted this matter, you dogface king,
Never care of whatsoever; threatening
To take this girl, I sweated as a prize,
Even, the soldiers have given me nice.

Have I plundered anything from the Troy?
Or any Trojan stronghold I destroyed?
But unlike the Akhaians who battered
Them and tossed, I choose to lift my manner.

I have seen more combats, in this deluge,
Hand and hand quarrels, I've seen in its grudge,
The win always come with the littlest rank,
And seldom they get reasonable flank.

For, in time of sharing the lots, you come
Getting more than a battalion must gram,
The greater share blunders in your pocket,
This, an injustice they must not forget.

Tired of your battles, worn out to retire,
On my ship I carry some trifle mire,
I too must get what is rightfully mine,
And carry to my shoulders this design.

Well then, I should make sail for home, by now,
Better these rest on my ship – I should know;
Why linger on you, waiting for my win?
Why make wealth for you, when they got nothing?"

To this, the high commander made reply:
"Desert! Go on, leave this place, like a fly,
If the wind tries to settle this desire,
Leave, for I shall not muse your heavy lyre.

Do you think I shall beg you to come back,
On this account, I wont – my heart's a rock!
The whole army honors me, king of Greeks,
The same with Zeus who knew all gifted tweaks.

Have you known an officer who hates me?
None to your sight! They're all honorary.
In battles, none act in faction but you,
Your rugged actions contested my shoe.

Be thankful for some god's favor are due,
I grant your wishes to leave, so adieu!
Sail, then, in your ship, and lord it over,
Your battalion of Myrmidons though rare.

Curse not, I have given nay – not at all,
Not for you, or for your anger, or your soul,
But here, I warn you, prince Akhilleus,
Listen to me: my words you can't refuse:

Khryseis, unto me is but required
By Phoibos Apollo, the master arched,
With this very ship she will be sent back,
And my people shall cease those who detract.

But that is not all, for I have one more,
Shall Briseis be summoned in my lore,
From your hut, she shall be taken my prize,

Though she's yours, she is mine, or otherwise.

That with these acts, I shall cause, you will know
That I am the king; and then, I must show,
And make your heart sick of her fair beauty,
Against those who seek equal place with me."

Thus Peleus' son weighed a sheerest pain,
His heart is stabbed by grief and pure disdain,
And in his unshorn chest, the lion roar
With shaking ire to unleash his terror.

Should he called upon death, blow his fiercest,
Draw the longsword from his hip, and the worst?
Mighty over the rest, and slay the king,
In a combat that's not far from coming.

O great son of Atreus, what's your fate?
Should death become early, or make it late?
O Akhilleus, hold your rage in time,
The hour is not proper for your crime.

For, from the heaven, the tumult has ceased,
While the blade has slept in its case deceased,
Slowly, from the sheath his anger is cast,
When the sky opens, and him alone surpassed.

Athena come to him from the high skies,
To plead not to waste his life when despised,
The goddess Hera, white-armed and glorious,
Sent her to appease their anger recluse.

Being fond of mighty, prevailing soul,

Hera must sustain them both overall,
That Akhilleus, to undraw his sword,
From Athena, these actions are her words.

Though visible to no one but him,
Akhilleus' red hair is gripped unseen,
Very near unto Agamemnon's blair,
Akhilleus knew something's in the air.

Like a startled felon, reaching for light,
He made a half turn to everybody's sight,
As soon as he saw her, he knew her grace,
Athena the goddess disbursed his race.

With eyes grey, blazing like fire in its core,
Time must have closed a little of its door,
Softly he speaks to her, but rapidly,
Rolling waters of river to the sea.

Akhilleus, mighty and bravely, said,
"O daughter of Zeus, who bear storms ahead,
Why are you here? To see his foolishness?
How he waste his sluggish words for my best?

What now, O Athena, shall I bring you,
The wisest of swords or the sheerest brew
Of Agamemnon's blood, boiled in a mud,
Thicken like curd and cursed against all odd.

Well then, my words I give you as a gift.
This time, and soon, shall he pay for this grief,
This king's honor is stirred like a poison,
His blood's the answer, in this quest alone.

Until his blood is razed to litter dosed,
The pain inside my heart may not recourse,
Should this longsword's blade upheave but no more,
Only when I know honor's still honor."

Athena the grey-eyed goddess speaks thus,
"Thy rage has reached the mountain Olympus,
That Hera has sent me to check your blade
That it may not kill a king, as you said.

From heaven I came, therefore, listen thou,
If you ever ascribe, then you may know,
The queen of heaven, to both of you, fond,
Would break in to cease your ravaging hand.

I said therefore, Enough! Then Break away,
This combat is an oaf to a black day,
A curse to people, a slant to your name,
What infamy has made thus in this game?

Two souls that Hera are fond of should stay,
Or otherwise, your life would gone astray.
Stay your hands once again to thy sword hilt,
And thou shall not this day in blood atilt.

Instead, use lashing words and raging notes,
That people may heard what manner to quote,
What fate this conversation leads must be,
Tell him his fate, and it shall therefore be.

My promise I give, and it will be kept,
Thy victory shall be three times adept,

In season due, this winning shall attain,
Worry nothing, just let this matter wane.

Such, as then, your requital lead enhance,
For his pride, against his arrogance,
Just that you have to listen, to my say,
Hold your hand still, and ardently obey."

The great runner, Akhilleus, answered,
"Nothing for it, goddess, should lead me dead,
When two immortals speak, a man should learn
To comply with reverence, in a stern.

To submit in aye though his heart burst out,
To listen though his very soul feels doubt,
Just as well as to honor our god's will
That they may honor ours what needs to fill."

On this, he stayed, awestruck in her promise,
His massive hand rests assure at his peace,
On the silver pommel, his hand silence,
And the blade slid back to repose; perchance

His soul in submission is lead at height
On her bidding, he composed himself right,
Then, off to Olympus, gaining the air,
She went like a wind leaving this affair.

With other divine, where she joined the rest,
In the powers of heaven she is blest,
It's now upon him to contain his choose,
To follow himself or the gods with Zeus!

So, in oath, the son of Peleus, curse,
With words lashing like whirlwind in its worst,
His anger ride eight horses astounding,
To Agamemnon, he said defying:

"O your black heart runs like an antelope,
March with a sack of wine against thy hope,
The cur in your eyes is blunt and blindfold,
The fate in your hands no one can behold.

Where is your kidney, strength in it composed?
You cannot buckle in it if you boast,
No armor may save you the future seen,
Not a troop will deliver you to win.

Seven of your mighty soldiers can't stand
In the ways of the gods, not one demands,
Oh no, death lingers very near lying
And it would not come to me! This, I sing,

Safer be with the gods, within my arm,
Is it not nobler to stay in their warm?
And feel that you are gods the same as them?
To get one man's prize that you rob and claim?

Leech! Your heart is a leech sucking but trash,
For you stand up against justice; the clash
Between us, I swear would not be done still,
The gods should render justice as I will.

Not one more soldier your arrogance will,
Not one more prize, your greedy soul may fill,
But long as I live shall I see you fall,

You are commander of the trash, that's all.

And here is what I say, an oath upon,
By this great staff, behold you wolfish man,
Leaf or shoot, it cannot sprout no longer,
Away from the log, it shall grow never.

Lopped away to the hills of timbered coal,
Your black heart in this manner firmly lull,
It cannot flower, no tints shall fill it,
No fragrance shall endow beauty for it!

Not even a sprout, for it is all peeled –
Peeled of bark and leaves; this, your fate shall fill,
Then, the staff shall be burned to ashes drawn,
And your time is passed as low trumpets blown.

Instead, Akhaian officers shall flay
The power that once your rude hands display,
As when they observe by the will of Zeus,
Not long your name exalted nor caroused.

Let this be what I swear be then, I swear
A day will come when every soldier wear
The name of Akhilleus on their head
Every Akhaian in my name is lead.

Shall they groan to let me go back instead,
And that is a joy, the high heaven has said,
That day shall drywood prevail no longer,
And flourish thus a mighty log must dare.

Driven though you are to the charcoaled hill,

As thousands of your men has perished skill,
Before the hands of Hektor the Trojan,
Thou shall perish as an ash before men.

Thus, you eat your heart out, for it is ripe
With remorse and pitiful cry; this life
Is simple: they who in dishonor, trashed,
Must end or his dishonor left unwashed.

For the bravest of the Akhaian soul,
Thou concluded wise; but it is your fall
That I waited before I shall begin
To laugh happily and festive within."

Hurled he the staff, studded nails and gold,
Before him against the ground thus behold,
As he sat on the ground, mocking in fury
The heart of Agamemnon to thee.

He looked across him, in sheerest recourse,
And Akhilleus in a jest restores,
Two fires, two rocks, against each other's fall,
Two blood boiling at each other's dark gall.

Nestor, the gifted orator, arose
In eloquence and wit must he composed,
For the sake of both men, he dispose fear,
And speak clearly the wisdom to his peer.

Of arguments sweeter than honey heard,
Rolled in his tongue the fruit of divine word,
In his tongue were noble truths gain attend,
He stand to fill the hall to such amend;

By now, two generations he outlived,
In aged wisdom and in Pylos conceived,
The third he ruled still; in such reply bounds,
A reproof to favor both men astounds:

"A black day, this is! A dreaded tears, ploy!
For the Akhaians to mourn and a foolish joy,
For how glad Priam and his sons would be,
And all the Trojans if they come to see,

Wild in joy they have to be: seeing that
Lashing words, truculent, in boiling hot,
If these comes with the wind, they shall have feast,
For between you there is none at the least.

How happy Priam be hearing all these?
And the whole Akhaian army their bliss?
What comes next after these prevailing feud,
Death and blood, or reign after someone's rude?

Agamemnon, chief in council you are,
Akhilleus, foremost soldier you are.
Listen true – your attention lend me with,
An aged man is advanced in spirit.

Both of you, younger men than my age was,
Must listen carefully for this, I must,
And in my time, greater men have I known
And listen to my words, neglecting none.

Men, who in mighty splendor reign, the same,
But I have never seen them more again,

The Lord Marshall Dryas, Peiritoös,
The mighty Kaineus and Exadios!

Of Polyphemos, and the great Theseus -
The son of Aigeus! A man like Zeus,
Yet mortal they are, immortal they stand,
Mighty among mighty, man among men!

These, I speak of champions among the earth,
Lest one great spirit subside, it may dearth,
They fought other champions – O here and there,
Thus exalted their victories so rare.

Curses of blood with wildest things unknown,
On mountains and places where they alone,
Great centaurs whom they broke, pierced, and
shattered,
These mighty titans they overpowered.

Among these men, I say, I've got my place,
When I sailed out to Pylos, I will taste
The sacred nectar of their fate, bestowed,
And alas, they called for me and honored.

I taught them, and had my hands among them,
Yet not one man on earth alive can claim
That they may stand against these men of fame,
But, I say, they listened first on my name

And my reasoning they took for advice,
With their victories, there is no surprise!
Well then, you two, listened to me the same,
It's far better than raze each other's name.

Lord Agamemnon, do not deprive
The girl to him, abandon this contrive,
The army thus allotted her to him,
This, you should comply for you, it's grim.

Akhilleus, on the other part, cast
No defiance to the king, or against,
No man vies in honor with him who holds,
Authority over what Zeus beholds.

You have more prowess, for Thetis bore you,
A goddess of the waters in thy lieu,
Yet his power over men exceeds yours,
For he is the King and Captain of yours.

But Agamemnon, get off with this ire,
And cool aside with both of your desires,
I beg relentless for Akhilleus,
Knowing him for victory shall he choose:

A sea wall for Akhaians he shall be,
In the black waters of war by this sea,
Abhor thy rages, both of you, unite,
There is Priam's army for us to fight!"

Then Lord Agamemnon answered the man,
"Fairly you say, sir, all of it I stand,
I honor these words from you everytime,
May these words be – in this place, in this time.

But this man's ambition we knew from start
Is to lead, and lord over, my own part!

Rule the army under my staff and rod,
Rule the Akhaians, and even the gods!

Should we take orders from him as he want?
For, if the gods immortal made him dand',
A spearman perhaps, have they put a shame
On his lips, and on their greater name?!"

Akhilleus interrupted, he said:
"Poltroon! What a poltroon thou art instead,
How lily-livered I should be called, nay,
If I knuckled under to all you say?

I dare, give your commands to someone else,
But not me! Or, knock down all worthy hells
For the sake of portraying king enough,
The whole Greek army, on your back, might laugh!

One more thing, I tell you this, listen well,
And think over, think hundred times, I dwell
In honor and not in kingly power,
But this time, for this girl, shall I not dare

Wrangle with you or anyone, I say,
Though I am robbed of what was my good stay,
But that is all, your poltroon hands can get,
Alongside my black ship, you should forget.

If against my will, you or your men play
Foul things, I suppose, then you make my day,
Try it! Hear this everyone; in this spear,
Your hot blood blackens instant; I'm sincere!"

So strong their words against each other's curse,
Face to face, they quarreled, against and worst,
Until they broke off the ships assembly,
And muster their way toward Aegean sea:

Akhilleus made his way to his own place,
With his squadron unto his quarter haste,
Patroklos, by his side, and companions,
Easing Akhilleus' dispositions.

Agamemnon thus launch a ship to make
An offering for the gods, he must take;
Twenty oarsmen he assigned for the task,
And loaded beasts for sacrifice. Alas,

He set Khryseis aboard in his ship,
In all her loveliness and beauty gripped;
The versatile Odysseus took the deck
And, all oars ready to thump the heck.

They pushed forward out into the waters,
And made their sacrifices; the troops
Were ordered to camp and offer their rites
Full-tally hekatombs they'll bid inspite.

Yet burned they pursue the gifts of honor
For Apollo; the barren surf dolors
And the savor curled in crooked smoke fro,
Toward the heaven, these gifts made it raw.

That was the day's labor in the army.
Agamemnon kept his threat candidly,
Afterwards, he acted upon, and called

Eurybates and Talthybios bold.

To these, his first aides and criers, said he,
"Both of you, to Akhilleus, must see
 And take his charming Briseis by hand,
And bring her to me. Do you understand?

Thus if he hesitates to give her right,
I'll be there with my bravest men of might,
In force shall I take her that he must know
I am the king, the more for him a gall.

So go along!" Off they went their way ward,
But for those who fear hid like scabbard,
They got no stomach to see what it brings,
Or what calumny is fated their wings!

To the waste sea, the barren coast shingle,
Grit to the eyes of cowards some, mingle,
Took shelters to the Myrmidons and rest,
But the two continue to walk their best.

Not far from his great black ship, he was found,
The prince in the open, seated; the sound
Of their coming is a cheerless sight though,
To Akhilleus, the promise must grow.

Shamefast Eurybates to him must ask,
and pale with fear Talthybios the task,
Yet they stood without a word to the prince,
Waiting what seawater afterwards rinse.

But he knew what they felt, and called them out:

"Peace to you, criers and couriers, a-couth,
Workers of Zeus and men! You come forward,
Not one thing I have against you on-guard.

Agamemnon is the man who sent thee
For my charming Briseis of beauty,
Here then, Patroklos, bring the girl at once,
And give her to these men as is, I must.

Let them both be witnesses before gods,
Who live in eternal bliss, wits, and scuds,
As before men who took their share of rest,
Including this harsh and greedy king-pest.

That, ever a need for me arises,
To keep the Akhaians and the whole rest
From black defeat and ruin, I shall not
Come to think I have hands, or part, or plot.

Neither a thought must I have to help thee,
On your land, or on battles of the sea."
Patroklos gave Briseis to them as they bid,
And went their way over the kingly greed.

Yet Briseis doubtful against her feel,
Loathing to go, her beauty rests instill,
Akhilleus wept, leaving hastily,
Felt the grit of loneliness from the sea.

He made his way to the shore and scan it,
By the grey waves and colors underneath,
Often he spread his arms for prayer deep
Unto his mother Tethis, in this keep:

"O mother, Tethis, goddess from the sea,
Thou bore me with life, though brief it be,
Honor at least from Zeus who storms the sky,
To thee I call my due, and rectify.

He gives me precious little, I speak not!
See me, Agamemnon mortified at!
He has my prize by his own whimsy greed,
Against myself who's mother-goddess feed!"

Eyes wet with tears, in sorry plea, he spoke,
And his mother heard him through the green loch,
Where his old father Poseidon lolled by,
She glides unto the water, not so high,

To sit down before his son in tears, she
Fondle him and said: "Child, why weep thou free,
What grief is this that matters you the most?
Out with it, tell, I too must know the cause?"

Akhilleus, fast in battle and rage
As a lion groans, and said: "Why should wage
I to tell you what you already know?
That thing I must get over made me low.

We sail the waters, raiding fiercely strong,
And took like a menacing storm along
The ancient town of Eëtion called Thebes,
By its land plundering down to ashes.

The slaves we counted head after head on,
Measured the spoils away this wealthy town,

Then, just as the division, later, comes,
The measure for me seems not right. The sums

Of her beauty, the young girl Khryseis,
Given to the king afterwards; then priest
Of Apollo, the father of the lass
Came to bring greater ransoms unencompass.

The priest of the Archer God, for her came
To the beachhead, we Akhaians ashamed,
He had the god's white bands to speak with us,
On a golden staff, asking grace we must.

The Atreidai commanders heard and fell
That the whole army in unison dwell:
'Behave well to the priest! Take the ransom!'
But like deaf, not would he, Agamemnon.

He went 'gainst the priest's desire cruelly
And drive the man off his face brutally,
Away the priest gone in grief and anger,
Yet Apollo cared, heed to his prayer.

What happens is that black bolt of plagues came
Flying openly to the Argives shame,
The priest's prayer Apollo heard befall,
To the Akhaian army's barren soul.

I said thus to him, 'Lo, appease the god!'
But he would not listen, that brutish wad,
Threatened your son two matters I cried for,
And what he threatened passed, and made me sore.

His threats are done: one girl the army gave
He has taken against my will forbade,
The young girl Khryseis for a good prize,
Agamemnon has taken compromise.

The other one, just now, from my hut, name
Briseis, a prize given for me; Shame
To that harsh poltroon, I should but stand it,
For say a greater prize is mine would fit.

If you choose to stand by me, O mother,
Go to Olympos, glorious mountain there,
By word or deed, thou hast served him better
And I heard you still tell it much brighter.

Thus, that time tremble, lurking silent mood,
When in the heavens not quiet understood,
When you alone shielded the son of Time,
It would be Kronos' gladness in its prime.

From peril aheight against their curses,
And disgrace against the gods menaces,
When against Pallas Athena thou shield,
Against Hera and Poseidon thou yield!

These gods who wish Zeus in iron bound all,
You alone freed him from that bondage brawl,
And called up to Olympus hastily
Aigaion, called Briareus, on lee.

This, the giant with a hundred arms, say,
More powerful than his old father gray,
Down he sat by the side of Zeus to slay

Any gods that come near, a corrupt prey.

With glory in that place, that titan rang,
The gods fear him, O Aigaios' deep twang,
Not one afterwards wished to manacle
This son of Kronos unto debacle.

Remind him of these things, mother Tethys,
To his knees, cling to his good vanities,
If to the Trojan, he take side, and roll
The Akhaians back to the water's gall,

Back to the ship with slaughter and disdain,
All the troops may savor what their king rein,
In madness he shall grew, and assert lose,
When he dishonored me amidst the cost!

Peerless among the Akhaians am I,
Son of the goddess, waters is thy vie;
Listen to your son, to his heart bestow
That made him woeful over that king's glow!"

Filling her eyes in tears, she answered thus,
"Alas, my child, given to thee, why must
I rear you, doomed before the day of light?
Let me take this matter, I say despite.

But be serene, not this beachhead alone
Provides you the length of time of your own,
The siege may cost lives, Oh early death may,
 Oh broken heart for me – I must repay!

Destiny, I have given your darkness,

That I bore you to this evil commence!
But what you wish shall I propose to Zeus,
Lord of the lightning, against that king's ruse.

Shall I go up there, to the snow-bound glare,
With hope of consent, on his presence dare,
Be quiet now, my child, guard on your ship,
Keep your anger light against mortal whip,

The army thou shall neglect, quit the war!
Last night, by the way, Zeus made himself far,
To the shore of Ocean, along a feast
With the Sunburned, and the gods at his ease.

In twelve days, his return shall tone my luck,
When at Olympos, he must rest his back,
Then, shall I cross his bronze doorsill and take
His knees. I trust I move him as he wake."

Thetis left her son Akhilleus strong
Yet still wanting for her girl's sweetly song!
That girl that they wrested for him a prize,
To Agamemnon's greed, and lashing vice.

Meanwhile, Odysseus, the fair general,
Came to Khryses, the priest to deem their soul,
With offerings in shipload, as the same,
And Khryseis, the most precious of dame.

Their ship entered the harbor deep, and furled
The sail and ease their stay; unbent they hurled
The mast down quick and soft into a rest,
And rowed her to a mooring undetest'd.

The bow-stones dropped, they tied up stern, released,
And all stepped down into the wash in peace,
Into the receding tide, their hearts ebb
In serene intonation they deserve.

The cattle rite, they offer to the Arch',
And Khryseis out of the ship embarked,
Odysseus, the great tactician led her
To her father's hands, purity, and care.

To the altar, he said, reneging not:
"Khryses, as Agamemnon's envoy, at
This flash we recompense to bring your child,
Pure the same without chide or has had wild.

And to great Apollo, a hekatomb,
Given under Danaän's name; our doom
We trust to placate your lord god to cease
Down the pain and sorrow in our army kissed."

So Odysseus delivered the young lass,
And her father the priest received at last
The child so dear to him, his only bliss,
Less to wait, the rite's handed by the priest.

To hasten the offering to the god,
Led blameless bullocks to the altar pad,
Around they go encircling the piecemeal,
Rinsed their hands, and delved with the sacred kill.

With baskets of barley, and ornaments,
The rite is cast by the old priest Khryses,

He prayed: "Oh hear thee, master of the silver bow,
Protector of Tenedos, on our low.

In my prayers thou listened once before,
And now I ask for Akhaian's restore,
Thou honored me, and punished them for me,
Now, let my wish come true, that I may see,

Turn away the plague to these army now,
Dearest Khryseis returned in our vow,
O Apollo, to the Danaäns, flee
Thy pestilence and plague, I pray to thee!"

This petition, Apollo heard as well,
For the priest's heart in sincerity dwell,
After the prayers sung, and said their wish,
And the barley strewn in the air unleashed,

The priests trained in sacrificing they held
The bullocks with a knife on its neck; spelled
Some words, and flayed the carcass and the meat,
Cutting out joints and the carrion neat.

These they enclosed in its two-layered fat,
Folded and with raw strips of flesh on that;
Then the priest burn the cloven faggots all
As wine wetted its mass, the present's call.

Around the priest stood young men in their sage,
With five-tined forks to subdue the ready wage,
The vitals were tasted, and joints consumed,
Apollo's forgiveness therefore assumed.

They sliced the chines and quarter for the meat,
Roasted them evenly and drew the heat,
The meal they prepared for all the work's done,
Apollo's curse away with Danaäns!

They feasted to their heart's passion instead
And made desire for more wine ahead,
They drink the wine in receding hustle,
And fortified themselves in bewilder.

Then young men filled their winebowls to its rim,
And the good wine flow in its mouth and brim,
In every cup, the god is praised aheight,
Every songs rose clear and strong as it might,

Until the day's end, Apollo's name's praised
The 'One-Who-Keeps-the-Plague-Afar,' they graced,
The listening god took joy of this feast,
And merry cheers skyward to get him pleased.

The sun went down, thus lingering night came,
In the darkness of the night, dreams they claim,
At last Odysseus men lay down to rest
Under the stern hawser, they line their best.

The Dawn spreads out, the stars mingle in vain,
Colors and beauty in the sky is plain,
Fingers of time rose, as the sea recalls,
For them to return back their valiant roles!

To the great sea they turned in steadfast speed,
Apollo, by the way, blew the high wind,
Unto the mast they woke, the canvas out,

The bellying sail, to the wind is caught.

Foaming darkest, blue wave upon their way,
The waters sang backward that early day,
The running ships rampage against the sea,
Till they went offshore to their courtesy,

Here they put in and hauled the black ship high,
Far from the sand, embraced with timbers lie,
And then disbanded, each to their own hut,
The Akhaians snatched bright allured and fat.

Meanwhile, unstirred and straight in his way thus
The son of Peleus, athlete to gods,
His smoldering heart unsurpassed wall,
Waits for his ship; and for him, that is all.

In the assembly of emulous men
He would not dare enter, neither his men,
Nor ever go to that harsh king's war greed,
Though the army his valor is in need.

In silence, his breast stale in idleness,
Missing the cries of battle and the rest,
In such a slumbering soul, the warrior losts
His name among the list of the utmosts.

Now, remembering Zeus, twelve days has passed,
The god who lives forever, back at last,
To Olympos, his power reign supreme,
Tethys has come there to serve his son's whim.

In her mind, the mission should give way bright,

Like the dawn rising from a misty night
Of the sea, clouds soared feathers and lofty,
In the heaven to Olympos' beauty.

Zeus with massive brows of grey-witted feats,
Apart yet handsome in the olden seats,
Thus enthroned the chief god in great splendor,
She slips down before him, pleads her favor.

Her left hand on his knees, wanting his say,
Her right hand cupping his chin in her way,
She made her plea a dolorous denote,
Thus: "O Father Zeus, high glory I quote,

If ever amidst immortal regrade
By word or deed I have served your bade,
Seek for your maid's honor, Akhilleus,
His doom is a rumble I did not choose.

That Lord Marshall Agamemnon stands high
Against my son whose prize was deprived, Why
This brooding fate comes to him in a guise,
While that harsh king's favor dwells his own lies?

That king highlanded my son to the low,
And his threats subdued the tears in my glow,
The king gets the prize that should be my son's,
And his mother's cry, hear my summons.

Thou can make him pay for it, profound god,
Lend the Trojans power and mighty rod,
Until Akhaians call upon my son
And heap new honor agreed to this plan."

Her words are done, yet a silence remain,
The gatherer of clouds for times attain,
No words is spoken, neither a sigh,
He remained silent, and she don't know why.

Tethis clung to his knees, and spoke once more:
"Give thy infallible words to restore
The glory of my son; O bow your head!
Are you afraid to see where this should lead?

That though I am lowly among the gods,
Thou hast provide me an answer? It's odds:
Your esteem against me has come to low,
Since when this happen, hence I've never know."

Greatly disturbed, Lord Zeus said, "Lo, it is!
Drawing trouble on me and Hera's peace,
Sooner or later, she will be at me
Scolding all the day long for this pleading.

Even as matters stand nay, she'll invoke
What this content of your say. Now, you walk
Away before she comes here to hear this,
But worry not, I'll arrange as you please.

Here, let me bow my head for your content,
To see me bound by this; now, clear thy wept,
My words are irrevocable and true,
Consider it effective just for you!

Shall I nod my head now: and it is done."
His ponderous black brows in this bent down,

The locks of ambrosia hued to his head,
Swung over as whole Olympos talk dead.

After this, they parted: misty Tethis
From the glittering Olympos made kiss
Good-bye, into the blue sea she returned,
And Zeus to his wonderful hall retired.

All the gods, however, rose from their seats,
In reverence before their father's feet,
Not one dared face him to ask about it,
Thus, in his throne, the immortals should fit.

But Hera knew, an interest wills him,
They thought she never saw Tethis, her grim,
That silvery-footed daughter she's called,
By the Old One of the sea! Yet, behold:

She inquired of Zeus Kronion, say: "Who
Is it this time, schemer, thou connive to?
Your ears, who has them now, making secrets
And plans unknown before I can forget?

Well, tell me your new plot that I may rest
My mind; favor me know it well and dressed."
The father of gods and men thus reply,
To Hera, his wife, in this manner, sigh:

"Hera, my providence you must not itch
To know. Rigorous they are, hard to stitch,
Though you are persistent, you must ease,
I advise not to harry me in this.

I choose, in this instance, to be alone;
And sick to entertain any question."
Lady Hera answered, wide eyes, she said:
"Majesty! I never 'harried' ahead,

Surely, you are free to speak when to tell
That that I must need, in the latter, dwell.
This time, however, I felt like disposed
When Tethis made her way to you, of course.

She might have lead you astray and awry,
By the daughter of Old One by the sea!
Just now at the daybreak, she came to you,
Take your knees, pleading something sore unto.

My guess is you bowed your head on her, dear,
In a solemn pact that she made but clear
For his son Akhilleus and his king,
That is, carnage to the Akhaian bring?

Zeus the gatherer of clouds awed, speaks thus:
"Marvelous! You and your guesses it must,
Nearing it, it may be. But, there is one
Thing you cannot do about; I, alone

Should and must. Sometimes it just estrange you
And know the gall afterwards in it too,
How it pleases me that your guesses true,
But what can you, dear, in this affair do?

Rather, sit down thy throne, and be still,
Obey my words not least of it, my will,
For none at Olympos may come to aide

When my hands lay upon you, when I said."

At this, the wide-eyed Hera, tremble down,
And sat quiet still, bent her will to one,
At the hall of Zeus, all gods were sullen,
Looked askance by this act in the heaven.

Hephaistos, master smithman, broke the air,
And doing kindness to the lady fair,
His mother Hera, snow-armed, and white,
Start'd to jewel his odes in this delight:

"Ah, what misery befall in this place,
When you two raise your voices in disgrace,
And fight over mortal creatures on earth?
Gods are we, and in eternity's birth.

This is more than enough already, dear,
To hear thy noisy bickering is near?
What pleasure can we, in this affair gain,
When we triumph in someone else's main,

But err in your own house with tears and wane?
What pleasure can a dinner give and reign
If the other hands touch baser things 'stead?
Would we ever finish to dine ahead?

To Mother, my advice is, make up with,
Or he'll thunder our feast to a mere bits.
You know he can shock us right this instance,
With lightning bolts and a thunderous dance.

His power reigns supreme! Oh, soothe him please,

Take a soft tone, make his anger appease.
Then, all Olympos might gather graces,
And he'll be pacified again and rest."

He lurched up as he spoke, and held some wine,
Out to her, a double-handed glass-wine,
And said: "Dear Mother, patience thou be strong,
Hold your tongue of unworthy beguiled song.

This, you may not upset him; I would not
Want to see you battered by him for that.
If it does, it would hurt me, shall I cry,
For I could not help you a bit, I pray.

One time, I came to oppose Father Zeus,
And he held one of my foot as he boost
The speed to flung me over sky ward,
And there I went: relentless from the start,

Not falling deep until the sun sets down,
I soared all day, and dropped at Lemnos town,
I was nearly dead, but the people nursed,
A fallen god they cared against his curse."

Hephaistos made her mother smile, at last,
Hera took the wine-glass on him steadfast,
Then, dipping from the winebowl, round he went,
Serving the other gods from right to left,

On ambrosial nectar of sweet delight.
And quenchless laughter broke along their plight,
When their beloved parents make it up,
And Hephaistos wheezing a thousand clap.

So all day long, until the sun went down
They went on feasting until the stars frown,
To their hearts' desire, their wine is enough,
Ten thousand jesters and their countless laugh.

So did Apollo's harp held flawless sound,
With heaven's songs in choiring antiphon,
All the Muses sang in joyous music,
Olympos' shines brighter, higher, and chic.

And when the shining sun in the west, arched,
They turned homeward each one to their own hark,
The bandy-legged smith, does wonders too,
Fashioned their rooms with crafts in various hue.

Zeus, the lord of storm and lightning, retired
And shut his eyes where sweet sleep is desired,
And at his side lay Hera, honey fair,
The so-called Goddess of the Golden Chair.*

Book II
MUSTERING OF FORCES

In deep slumber, the gods slept in heaven,
So those who fought at Troy the night ascend,
Horse-handlers, charioteers in splendor gained
Yet defenseless when the languor attained.

To all gods slumbering, except mighty Zeus
Who has power over the bed refused,
Pondered the whole night how to exalt thus,
O Akhilleus, half-water, half-dust!

His question as to how to destroy fleet
Unto the waters they reside and seat?
In windrows strong, or some calamity,
To promote the son of Tethis he be.

He thought that night abstruse a fatal dream
To Agamemnon's plan and unsaid whim,
In darkness reached the ale of the harsh king,
To Dream, he said: "Thou sinister Dream, bring

Yourself down amidst the fast ships of fate
Unto Akhaian army, enter the garish gate
Of Agamemnon's head, and tell him neigh,
As I commanded you, point by point, say:

Let him prepare the carls of Akhaia
To fight at once! Now, he may take triumph
Unto Trojans, if he tailed this instruct,
The Olympians, tell him, not out of track,

And of two minds no longer – do the act!
Hera swayed them in banner red and dark,
The black days overhung tonight implore,

Wake, Agamemnon, and unleash the gore!"

At this, the dream left, carrying his word,
Serving in honor his majestic lord,
Descending swift as a whirlwind that night
Unto the long ships of Akhaian might.

And sought where Agamemnon lay and glare,
The son of Atreus, the kingly heir,
In his hut, he was found in pillows pair,
Drifted in the balm of deepest slumber.

Unto the marshall's comfort, standing still,
Dream took the shape, according to his will,
Ah, the form of Neleus' son, old Nestor,
For he revered his wisdom and valor.

Of all his peers, Nestor rank first to him,
So Dream speak softly wise, disguised as him:
"Sleeping, son of Atreus, tamer you
Of horses and wild beasts, wildering dew,

You should not sleep all night, captain of men,
Relentless thy duties, keep thee attend,
A great voice in you needs to he heard tonight,
A discussion of war should bring its light.

Follow me closely firm, I am from Zeus,
Messenger afar, yet thou he has choose,
'Prepare the troops', he said, without delay,
Take the spacious town of Troy in your way.

The Olympian god are two minds no longer,

Hera pleading swayed them all, and despair,
A victory for the Akhaian cause,
A defeat from Zeus to the Trojan host!

Hold on to this message before it's gone,
Remember these words to witness thy plan,
Forget not, as tides of day brings the sun,
When the blissful slumber is all but gone."

Therefore, Dream withdrew in his night alone,
Left the man envision what got his plan,
A thought to conquer Priam's Trojan prize,
Two mighty countries racing for sunrise!

What could lay ahead in the mind of Zeus
That he do not know? Is he all confused?
But mighty god was he, he must know all,
The shocks of combat when such act befall.

Of mighty Akhaian the waters swift,
Of mighty Trojan's arrows thus they lift!
The army of the Greeks against their wall,
The bloodshed's end is a desperate call.

Walking, he heard the dream voice, ringing loud
Capturing his thoughts, seizing him errand,
So he sat up straight, and pull his tunic,
A fresh one he never worn before. Seek

To brighten himself, his cloak he shook nice,
Tied his shining feet with a sandal size,
Then hung his baldric and longsword about,
And his staff on his hand, made his way out.

Pure Dawn had reached the might heaven side,
Olympos' beauty heralds Zeus to ride,
Along with the other gods this morning fed,
On heaven and earth, the assembly's led.

Lord Agamemnon his proud marshall call,
Met his clarion criers and tell their role,
To call Akahaia in full assembly,
For he must tell the coming injury!

The call shorn sang out like a rapid horse,
Quickly assembled the army, of course,
But first, alongside Nestor's army held
A council where his plan he kindly spelled.

This he put before them, saying: "Hear me,
Friends, for ages I have been with all thee,
A vision in a dream has come to me,
Down in slumber with the night starry,

A figure standing above my pillow
In height and bearing as Nestor would show,
The messenger said unto me, I say,
If memory is right, then in this way:

 "Sleeping, son of Atreus, tamer you
Of horses and wild beasts, wildering dew,
You should not sleep all night, captain of men,
Relentless thy duties, keep thee attend,

A great voice in you needs to he heard tonight,
A discussion of war should bring its light."

Thus, I woke up early to think of these
And consult before your wise, gentle peers.

"Follow me closely firm, I am from Zeus,
Messenger afar, yet thou he has choose,
'Prepare the troops', he said, without delay,
Take the spacious town of Troy in your way.

The Olympian god are two minds no longer,
Hera pleading swayed them all, and despair,
A victory for the Akhaian cause,
A defeat from Zeus to the Trojan host!

Hold on to this message before it's gone,
Remember these words to witness thy plan,
Forget not, as tides of day brings the sun,
When the blissful slumber is all but gone."

Then, dream like a bird swiftly flew away
A phantasm with golden news today!
Thus, slumber left me, thinking all the night,
Even after the dawn, within this light!

Look to it then, we arm our troops to war,
But let me test first – that I may not scar,
Such as old custom harangued in my vest,
That I may rest assured of all the rest.

What I propose to launch ships to waters,
Flight in the silver-tone wash; Hold them verse
Speaking glory unto each one's own brave,
That I may rest assured, of these I crave."

How concisely he told his curious plan,
And took his seat, holding his eyes a span,
Now stood old Nestor of the sandy shore
Of Pylos, in anticipation, more:

"Friends, lords, and captains of the Argives arm,
If other men told this dream, don't becharmed,
A fiction, that is. We should call it thus,
But he who saw the vision is, alas,

Our king! Up with you, mighty captains sing,
But we'll put the men in arms a-flaring."
On this, the council being led, unite,
The counselors rose and obeyed his right.

Then, thick as bees in a honeycomb swung,
The army awaits their fateful harangue,
Troops still turning out, swarms in multitude,
Facing the mountain grand, the interlude

Resounds; yet endlessly pouring forth, fair,
Countless army, strong, within the bright air!
Like bees uncountable from ships and huts,
A regiment so thick, the raincloud shuts.

Rumors abound of such a crier sent
From Zeus' heaven, the sacred message went,
Turmoil grew in the great field they entered,
And sat down, clangorous crowd, hubbub aired.

Now, nine men, criers, shouted in their midst,
"Quiet! Quiet! Attention! Our king needs…"
Then, in respect or fear, the army heard,

Their seats are taken, and hushed their din; Weird

Though something great is coming forth redeem,
As when Lord Agamemnon before them,
Rose in kingly splendor holding the staff
That god-smith Hephaistos took pain and rough.

It was a gift passed 'long, fashioned and rare,
From the son of Kronos, from Zeus with care,
Who gave it to the pathfinder Hermes,
Whom he gave to Pelops, the chariot's ease.

Pelops to Atreus, the father king,
Who gave it to the shepherd Thyestes bring,
Who gave it to Agamemnon, the lord
And Marshall of the many islands, Argos.

The very same man leading the army,
Who spoke out among the Argives was he:
"Friends, fighters, comrades of this mighty band,
Listen to my words, king I of this land!

Companions of Ares, I shall bespeak
The son of Kronos entangled trick,
In cruel folly, O errant god! He
Promised that I should not sail, solemnly,

Before I stormed the inner town of Troy,
And make myself a lost lonely boy!
But crookedness and duplicity is
This whole matter in my dream madness fixed.

But calls me return to Argos beaten

On our powerful throne, all dust and smitten,
Unto great state of Peloponnesus,
Shall I embark after many losses,

This might be his pleasure and his good will,
Who knows why, comrades, or what potions kill,
That many a great town we have destroyed,
And will destroy, what more is left for Troy?

But being, in power high, lacking not,
Allow this shameful enact through his plot?
What should be heard by future men ahead,
That we're strong yet our arms are useless dread?

Thus, we made long years of war for nothing,
Days and nights in a fuzz, we're for fighting,
Yet to an end of what? We had the odds
Thereof, culminating titans and gods!

The odds? – if Akhaians and Trojans hold
A truce and a tally just like the old,
On one side the native Trojans effect,
And on the others, Akhaians, reflect,

If we drawn up muster a squads of ten,
And each squad took one Trojan for our men,
As steward, many squads are left unserved,
I tell you, they are always outnumbered.

The men of Akhaia in power lift,
Against those whose home is a Trojan sift.
But, tame your hearts, listen as I open
One folly that we'll take against these men,

But they abound many Asian allies,
Many cities will come for their reprised,
If one nation tries to plunder great Troy,
And repeatedly fall under this ploy,

Then what is left for us to know unless
Akhaian soldiers live in foolishness?
Under great Zeus, nine years fruitless gain,
Making ships a rotten gone in thy lane,

Affray old tackle, nasty days aroused,
Yet our children and wives back in our house,
Be still in silence when we would return,
Tears and murmuring sea our compass learned!

And our mission has not gain its tone,
Making bloodsheds all over, well and done,
So in this, I should say, Retreat! Embark
For our fatherland, hope is not our lark!"

The army's heart leapt in a quick response,
Off their gilded breasts, happiness perchance,
Rank and file, without warning of his plan,
The height of gladness thus embraced all men.

The ground began to surge the swarm of bees,
Swelling the meadows and the verdant hills,
On dark Ikarian deeps the silence blurred,
Wandering with winds blown by the great god.

By south and east, the virtue of his mouth,
From Zeus' lungs, the inexorable cloud-land!

The field of standing grain puffed 'gainst the west,
Crossing its billows, the vapors attest,

And the tasseled ears of fate, run them down,
Bent and tossed, the army's assembled sons,
In shouts confusing, and hail unworthy,
Began to unscramble their tidal glory.

High in the air, the clouds presume appears,
Scuffling rose in the midair like some spears,
Commands the general thus back and forth,
Brace themselves in the lost, they must abort.

Yet, they manned the cable, and hauled their ships,
Black spots in the salt immortal seas! Ships
Of black, and timbered strong, the launch is prime,
They gonna go home though the winds sublime.

Thus, overriding their destiny lies
The Argives went homeward, full mechanized,
Had Hera resorted to Athena,
The army to their homeland, Akhaia!

Hera to Athena, cried: "Athena,
These army went homeward to Akhaia!
Can you believe this, O tireless daughter
Of Zeus, the shields of clouds and rain thou bear!

Will they put out for home this way, my dear,
The Argives to the broad black sea of fear?
How on earth would they abandon Helen,
Princess of Argos, lady to Spartan?

Would they leave her unto king Priam's hand –
The boast and silver pride of all Trojan?
Helen, for whom Akhaians in thousand
Died and suffer distant off their homeland?

Ah dear, go down to these sergeants-at-arms,
In your mild way dissuade them, one by one,
From hauling out their graceful ships to sea,
O Athena, glide down right now, and see…!"

Then, grey-eyed goddess Athena obeyed,
Diving swifter than the wind, to persuade,
Down the crest of Olympos, she get swayed,
To the ships long and strong, busied her bray.

There she found the strong belts of Odysseus
In stratagem, the peer of mighty Zeus,
Holding his ground, looking inward aghast,
He had not touched the prow nor his long ship's
mast,

For anguish filled him, torments, heart and soul,
And halting near him, the goddess befall,
And made the plea to him, saying: "Listen,
O son of Laertes, and gods olden,

Odysseus, master mariner-soldier,
Must all of you oar back in surge and mare,
Leave your destiny here for your country,
Come to think twice, this is the history,

Leaving Helen unto Priam's convert
Argive's grace is lost, The Trojan asserts

This a victory worth inscribing on stones,
And now, where is the wonder of your own?

Helen, for whom Akhaians' died and writhe,
Far from yourhomeland, your names thus achieved,
Nay, take heart, and go among them, for war
And dissuade them to understand your star!"

Each time he met an officer and rank,
He paused and in his ear, he said but frank:
"Don't be a fool! Should you not desert thee
The way a coward would, your come, halt thy flee!

You don't yet know what Agamemnon means!
Befooled not! He tested so courage wins,
Something punitive comes next, later on,
For not everyone heard his position.

Heaven forbid he cripple, in his rage,
And the army he commands long an age,
There is passion within kings we don't know,
They held power from Zeus that always grow!"

But when Odysseus met some common war
Bawling thus, they drove him back; As a jar
Of Mud, their valor retires for their home,
But the porcelains are better at some.

With staff and rod, he swung upon them, say:
"Fool! Go back, sit down, listen thee, I pray,
Unfit for soldiers as you are, weak lass,
Counting for nothing in this battle trust.

Should we wield the power of the king? Nay!
And any masters to no good to stay?
But let there be one commander for all,
One authority over us, I call.

With royal staff and precedence, he stands,
From Zeus' lightning, the son of Kronos hands,
Though crooked-minded his father it seems,
There is one to command our lives and dreams!"

So Odysseus went through his way, and lord
The army's heart for their king's prudent word,
And back to the assembly ground they streamed
From ships and huts their innumerable whims.

Roar aboard their hearts thus infinitive,
Just like the comber from the sea it lives,
On a majestic beach goes thundering
And subside as wall in their clamoring!

So all the ebb, receding quick, and fast,
Except to one man who's called Thersites,
A leaking soldier, blabbing, and clown-like,
Whose imprudence with his officer hike.

He, who though himself amusing to all,
The most obnoxious and a loathsome soul,
Who went to Troy with, fighting for glory,
And yet, himself has not a name to be.

A limping leg had he, bow-legged too,
With shoulders rounded above his chest; grew
A skull quiet conical, and a mangy mold,

Fuzzing sword whose sheenless blade cannot hold.

Odious to Akhilleus, this man was,
And hateful to Odysseus, that he must,
Having yapped at both, yammer many times,
But this time, had he berated his crimes,

To degrade the king is a furious haught,
Listen to his words, and judge what he got:
"Agamemnon! What must you groan about?
Come, O king, slumber not in your bronze hut!

What more can you gape and gawk after?
Bronzes fill your place, plentiful and fair,
Studded in glory thy name with honors loud,
And with the hottest girls, your vices bound.

Do we not hand them over to you – why?
Have you lack gold to insist a good lie?
A Trojan father will bring you golden bowls
In ransom for his boy! – though I, in growls

Of a pitiful man conceive, a slave,
Aye, like a prisoner on your conclave,
Without time and honor to fill my soul,
But hasten glory of a king and all.

Or a new woman to lie with, but nay,
Thou keep stowed away from us, as you may,
Is that your heart's desire, that's cloudy murk?
To send us back to war beneath thy lurk?

Comrades! Are you women of Akhaia?

Slaves you become for being an epah:
Easily tossed in the butter furnace hot,
Eaten as one will, bitten by his mouth.

I say, pull away from his soured desire,
Pull away for home, leave his burning fire,
His lust a monster, his girls in this beach,
Is this not enough a blood for a leech?

Should he find us indispensable here,
When his battles he drops us, it is clear,
Contemptuous was he to a man great
Twice his quality, he much offended.

By keeping Akhilleus woman snatched,
To this great hero, who else can he match?
But there's no bile to his blood, he let go,
And the reason remains a furtive blow!

Sir, if he withdrew his blade, come to think,
Would he not abuse a new man a blink?
If to that great warrior, he does bid foe,
Now, I wonder why, his army should woe!"

So boldly Thersites baited the king,
Without words, abruptly he felt exploding,
But poor Thersites, he just got bad dream,
Odysseus halted, glaring whims and grim:

"You spellbinder cheat! You bag of cursed wind!
Be still! Will you stand up again your din?
Such a ruckus alone in your head's firm,
It needs some screwing to fasten your dream.

For, of all who came here to siege for Troy,
I say no soldier is worst than you, boy.
Better not raise your voice, but laud thy king,
And rail your words right, or the worst it bring?

After these lies awake, nothing else does,
In your mind consist but a home you must,
We have no notion, none, what will come on,
What may turn out after this campaign's thrown?

Yet you bleat on, whining curses and lie,
Defaming your master – of all kings, why?
Because Danaän veterans gave him
Plentiful gifts of war? That's what it seems.

You sicken me! However, listen wise,
You open your ears with some good advice,
For, this promise I shall keep in my heart,
If I heard your voice, commit further start,

I hope Odysseus' head may be knocked loose
From his own shoulder, for I shall but choose
No longer to braid dear Telemakhos,
If I do not take hold of your abstruse.

And strip you to two or a thousand cuts,
Yes, even the shirts that hides your vile scuts!
From this assembly ground, your howling raised,
And whip you like a dog back to your place!"

At this, he struck him sharply with his staff
Against his ribs and shoulder it fell gruff,

The poor devil quailed, sorry for his pose,
And a welling tear fell from his compose.

A scarlet welt, swelling line in his skin,
Raised the golden-studded staff it would bring,
Against his back sprang out pain and the fear,
He cower like an imbecile in tears.

He wiped his eyes upon his arms a sore,
Odysseus mad at him, cease him implore,
The soldiers, for all their frustration cause,
Fell to laughing at the man's feeble dross.

One fellow, you might have heard, glancing say:
"What a clout that is! Wallop bashing prey!
A thousand times Odysseus made good works,
Thinking out ways to fight as the needs lurk.

This time though he's done the best deeds on war,
To capsize that poisonous clown afar,
By god, encircling miles around, shall bore
The brilliance that is his sole prize to wore.

The crowd took it that way, the poor man's ail,
But the raider of the cities unfail,
Mighty Odysseus with his staff proclaim,
For stood in his side, Athena's great name.

In the shape of a crier, calling thus:
"Silence!" that every man submit him pass,
On front rank, or rear alike, they may weight
What the tactician proposed his comrades.

He spoke: "Lord Agamemnon, Atreus' son,
My king, your troops are willing to undone,
What is spoken in behalf; rather wise
They commit to honor the war as prize,

That they may not leave for Argos and home
Until they plundered Troy! Though callow some
And wail the few for they're homesick as you,
Missing their wives and children as I do.

I grant this hardship tossing out passion,
But it builds another a richer zone,
I grant the urge to go – no more – afar
From home, and the savor they used to mar.

For one more month at sea, the raiders sick,
Of his ship, as gales and rising sea, Bricks
And waters and mud cannot serve their urge,
Delay not the war, delay not the surge!

As for ourselves, the ninth year came, so long
We keep this siege, the longer we do wrong,
No wonder at it, then: I cannot blame,
Why many become seasick in this game.

Ah but still, an utter shame, hindrance gives,
To stay long and go home empty Argives!
Hold on hard for a short time now, my friends,
This will structure to a beautiful end.

Come, sweat it out until at least we know
If Kalkhas made his prophecy a no,
Or if a yes, we would learn – so be it,

Only death can testify as we breathe.

One day, at Aulis, loaded, everyone,
A stage for Priam and his Trojan men,
With woe as spent, we gathered to their lose,
Through a fountain by the altar amused.

Performing sacrifices to the gods,
Under a dappled sycamore withstands,
The water welled up crystal shining,
And a great portent appear, as we sing.

A blood-red serpent whom Zeus himself sent,
Glides toward the light, blood-chilling and silent,
Beneath the altar entwined in a coil,
Swiftly spiraled the tree without a toil.

There were fledgling sparrows, some young and old,
In downy wings, and hunching feathers told,
Eight of which among the leaves utmost flew,
And the ninth being hatched, matched their sinew.

The serpent slid to the hatchlings devoured,
All pitiful, the blood-thirst of the hour,
The mother in shrilled distress tries her best
To catch the serpent whilst her wing unrest.

After the snake replete its thirst for blood,
The god who sent him turned an omen stud,
The serpent was turned into a black stone,
Hid him within the dark and silent stone.

This, clearly his work, the son of Kronos,

And we stood awed by it, on what might cause,
Seeing this augury of god had roam
So Kalkhas told the meaning of its pomp.

He said, 'Gentlemen of Akhaia, stay,
An omen has been given us today,
And a great one it is, granted by Zeus,
A promise inscrutable and obvious.

A promise long to be in fulfilment,
And fame will never die in that event,
Consider the snake devoured fledglings eight,
And the mother made nine, the serpent ate.

Nine are the years our army wage this war,
And the tenth, we shall have the Trojan par,
This, what Kalkhas explanation intends,
And see how it all could come true, my friends?

Hold out, then! Akahaians to thee attend!
Cause thy Trojan fall, behold beachhead wend!
Unto war we are! Unto Trojan lair!
Then, after this homeward our noble fair!"

A great shout from the Argives he received,
Echoed seven times around the longships,
To noble Odysseus words, they cried "Aye!"
Then Nestor, lord of Gerenia pray:

"Lamentable, the way thou acted lush,
Like boys and children sternly giving hush,
What will therefore come, so bring ours the war,
If that is so the proem of our stars!

What then, comrades, our pacts and oaths shall say,
'To the flames,' I heard your compact must gray,
'For, with battle plans, and soldierly vow,
The wine is pledged unmixed, until we draw.'

Once we stood, and honor this sacred deal,
Thus assures the trust we account and bill,
But if wrangling sounds and high words dispel,
Turn no remedy though we catch the hell!

Son of Atreus, be as you were, king,
Inflexible, obdurate, unbending,
Commit the troops to combat in your name,
Let the war for Troy deliver their shame!

And, let those few who take counsel apart,
Be cursed among Akhaian dread and wart.
They are victor nay, winning nothing sort,
They would sail Argos cowards and cohorts!

What great Zeus promised, be it true or false,
In the far reaches of Greece filled thy morse,
In Asia and all empires of the East,
This omen shall be an eye I behest.

I think, and I dare to say my belief,
That the power above us nodded, If
On that day the Argives put to the sea,
Their fast sailing ships be called cowardly.

But aboard thy fate, the Trojans appeal,
Mighty Akhaian army gladly seal'd,

For, mighty Zeus, forking in heaven rule,
This fateful sign our sages used for tool.

Therefore, press not our return on our land,
Before he beds down a Trojan wife; Laid
In the abundance of Spartan seeds,
To avenge what to fair Helen they didst.

If any would sooner die than to stay
Let him lay hand upon this ship, and pray,
He meets his death and doom before the rest,
Even before that glorious day attests!

My lord, persuade this achievement a hand,
What I am going to say is not fun,
A trifle plan, nor a toss aside, but
Something wisely we must marshall about.

Marshall the troops, divided by nation,
And then again by clans, in that fashion,
If you will do this, and carry out thus,
You may find out which captains stays with us.

Whose nation may be poltroons and swine-breed,
Which are valorous in word and deed!
On foot soldiers too, command this demand,
As each will fight before his noble clan!

Where clan shall make up units in this war,
You can discern how the siege went on far,
By men's will, their honor remained bestill,
Or faintheartedness and foolishness kill!"

Lord Agamemnon made reply: "Believe
Thee, sir, our victory is bright conceived,
The waters of the spring in the summer bring,
The fair wind of the zenith when gods sing!

O Father Zeus, give thee ten more of him,
Athena and Apollo, to thy hymn,
Priam's fortress then fall in just a day,
And touch our spoils of his royalty's play.

But Zeus the king of storms and lightning strike,
Brought misery upon me, I don't like,
Plunging into futile brawl, useless feuds,
I meant me and god-like Akhilleus!

We fought though, like enemies, in a burst,
Over a girl – and I gave anger first,
If we could ever think as one, comrade,
The Trojan's golden days will come to fade.

Your meal shall thou take, and shall wear thy shield,
Our time is prepared for combat; the chill
In your hearts, fade away, warriors and all,
There is no space for cowardice thy soul!

Make sure whetted thy arrows and spears sharp,
Slung well thy shields and armory un-warp,
Let every charioteer inspect their wheels
And put their mind on the war trumpet's shrills!

So bear yourselves as men of the battle,
For once you are there, there is none to call,
Not even the gods may listen to thee,

For the Olympians await this revelry.

Unless the night comes on, dissolving rage,
The lines of men wretchedly slaughtered wage,
The shield strap soaked sweat in your ribs and back,
On the spear shaft thy hands shall stiffen rock.

Thus, the horses shall drench in sweat and passed,
Either blood or sweat in thy car awash'd,
Thy wheels and bravery within might pull,
But there's only one life you cannot fool.

But let me see, one of you, willing to
Drop out around the ships, crying for two,
Hence he has no chance against a wild dog
Or a kite who fare a find another drag."

Being so dismissed, the Argives roared loud,
As when a loud wind came that roused the south,
In jutting point, a rock stood the habit,
Until the wind scatter around amidst.

So the soldiers in swarm scattered to rise
Unto their ships to send a smoke; the cries
Of waters, and waves shuttering, strongly,
Made the squads on their knees, in prayers see.

But first, to one of the gods immortal,
Resigned their bit and made his prayer call,
To keep away death from that day's fighting,
And ominous doom the Trojans are waiting.

As for Lord Agamemnon, commander

Chief of the Argives and Danaän's heir,
A fattened ox he chose for ablution,
For the glory of that day's condition.

To Zeus whom shall he oblate the old rite,
Calling around his senior captains might,
Lord of the Akhaian host, he called them,
The offering shall bless, the rite proclaim'd.

Of Nestor, then Lord Idomeneus,
Two lords Ajax, then son of Tydeus,
The sixth was great and mighty Odysseus,
The peer warcraft man of the storm-god Zeus!

Then Menelaos needs not summoning,
Lord of the warcry, his strength approving,
He who knew and shared his brother's duties,
These warlords gathered together the list.

Around the ox they stood, took the barley
Agamemnon pray on their behalf, say:
"O excellency, O majesty, Zeus,
Beyond the storm cloud, thy infinite truce!

Thou dwell in the air, let not the sun set
This day into the western gloom, forget
Not thy promise to tumble Priam's crown,
Exploding fires and shatters in his throne!

Let my bronze point rip unto Hektor's shirt,
And his breastplate broken into the dirt,
That I may slash his ribs, may throngs lie 'round
Him while he faces down, eating dry ground!"

But Zeus would not accomplish these dire foe,
He took the ox but added woe on woe!
That he must entreat the promise likewise,
Though he remained easy with what belies.

When prayers are said, the barley strewn spent,
They held the bullock for the knife and went,
Flayed unto its skin, cutting joints, and meat,
Wrapping in fat, two layers, folded neat.

To burn on cloven faggots, and the tripes they spit
To the broiled; when every joints done with meat,
And kidneys tasted, they quarter slice,
So chines and bellows on the smoke comprised.

The meal being served and prepared today
For the work done; they feasted till they slay
The meat and the drink on their plates and cups,
As lauds to Zeus' promise on their behalf.

Then Nestor spoke: "My Lord Excellency,
We shall do well if we do not tarry
Any longer, to ascribe Zeus' talent,
Put no ire on our arm's predicament.

Let criers among Akhaian soldiers
Muster the troops along the ship gutters,
And shall we pass together their bold line
To rouse their appetite a warring dine."

Then, Agamemnon turned at once, to call
The criers, send out the shrill down and all,

To all Akhaian troops the battle signed,
With their blood and hope thus homeward consigned.

The cry went out, and the men crowding mass,
Officers along their soldiers as just,
Swiftly down to form each unit and block,
A squadron of death, a swarm of bedrock.

The grey-eyed goddess Athena attends
To keep the pace of the army ascends,
Bearing her shield of storm and august cloud,
That shadows the army of death so proud.

She, whose golden-plaited tassels would worth,
Each a hekatomb, floated to and forth,
So down the ranks, the dazzling goddess guides,
To stir the attack, the blood odious ides.

Each men grew strong each step along the way,
And never quit any rumpus melee,
Lovelier than return these men askance,
Lovelier than sailing, they mind the chance.

As in forest dark and oblivious bites,
Measureless lore in the eyes of the scribes,
Such conflagration hails, blaze hellish pyre,
Of countless men in the burn of their mire.

The sores of death, the fire of the red glows,
Haste in the tomb, the infernal coal blows,
Now, the fiery lights a mile hosts in bronze,
Flashed like lightning, every smiting announced.

As migrating birds, nation by nation,
Wild geese in white and black coloration,
The arrow-throated cranes and swans over
Asia's meadowland and marshes lair.

Around the stream of Kaystrios, marching,
With giant flight and feathers glorying,
Their wings keep beating down in tumult high,
Verdant lands that echoes the battle cry!

Pinions that rare, minions of bidding claire,
Thy clarion smooth, in the rhythm snare,
Even so, nation by nation, flocking
Air, made their way bold enough a-marching!

Debauched upon wide Skamander's plain,
Wicked shelter of the heaven disdain,
Noises of thunder pent brashy and loud,
Gaudy soul trampling earth scanning the ground!

Under the horse's hooves, struck time's ardor,
They filled the flowering land enamored,
As countless as the leaves and blades of spring,
The army went a trod, thus advancing.

Buzzing clouds another, fevered flies floss,
That swarm the cattle of the summer moss,
When pails of milk splash, sour after the night,
So the army marched along thus recite.

But just as the herdsmen easily rift,
So they were marshalled side by side; what if
Like sheep mingling the pastured den, dispatch'd

The army towards a gleaning combat.

Agamemnon's lordly mien, seems like god,
Zeus' appearance, with his staff and rod,
He whose joy is the lightning and storm-cloud,
Oaken-waisted as Ares, the war god.

Like Poseidon's deep-chested form appears,
And as a great bull in majesty lears,
Tower supreme over the grazing herd,
This son of Atreus, his lordship conferred.

Tell me now, Muses, who dwell in heaven,
Olympos thy home, and thy great mountain,
As you are heavenly and everywhere,
And everything is known to thee a seer.

While the tales we have not heard you conceal
That this day may be the greatest reveal,
Unto Danaän lords this day shall keep,
In the scribes of their lore's immortal lips.

The rank and file, I shall not name within,
For I could not; but if I was given
Ten tongues and unfaltering voices gold,
In my memory and heart I shall told.

Unless the Muses, daughters of the gods,
Might recall all those who campaign the land
Of Troy; let me name only captains known
And number all the ships in this fashion:

Of the Boiotians – Penelos, Leitos,

Prothoenor, Lonios, and Arkiselaos
Were captains. The pride of various cities:
Men of stony town Hyria and Aulis.

Those who live in Skhoinos and the Skolos,
On and beyond the glens of Eteonos;
The dancing ground of Thespeia and Graia,
Of Mykalessos, and around Harma.

Eilesion, Erythai, Eleon,
Hyle, Okalea and Peteon;
And the compact Medeon city groves,
Kopai, Eutresis, Thisbe of the doves.

Those too of Koroneia and the land-grass
And town of Lower Thebes and Glisas,
Of Haliartos, and men of Plataia,
Glisas, city ringed with walls; and Nisa.

The great Ongkhestos where Poseidon hums,
And those of Arne, rich in purple rums,
The men of Mideia, and Arthedon,
All these had fifty ships for their great sons!

And hundred twenty Boiotian fighters
Came in every ships, vigorous soldiers,
Robust sons of great Boiotes in the sky,
To the Akhaian warlord's battle cry!

Their neighbors of Aspledon, then Minyan,
Orkhomenos, Askalaphos their captain,
With Ialmenos, both sons of Ares,
Conceived in Aktor's manor in a tryst,

The women's room above, came Ares hold,
Passing in silent brisk, no soul beholds,
Where the god secretly lay in the room.
Thirty ships these Minyans drew for Troy's doom.

Then, Phoikan in their turn lead by Shkedios
And Epistrophos, sons of Iphistos
Naubolides, the hero; Phoikans dwelling
In Kyparissos, rocky Pythio sing.

Holy Krisa, Panopeus and Daulis,
Near Hyamporeia, and Hyampolis,
And by the side of great Kephisos,
Or in Lilaia, where the river is close.

Forty black ships had crossed the sea with these,
Who drew the company of Boiotes,
And armed themselves in honor and in pride,
Sons of Ares the same the Boiotians ride.

The Lokrians had Ajax as commander,
Oileus's son, this Ajax known as Short – compared
To Ajax Telamonios – who being
Neither tall nor great against his breeding.

A corselet of linen he wore; beware:
He out-thrown Hellenes and Akhaian spear,
His were Lokrians who live at Kynos,
And men of Opoeis and Kalliaros.

The pretty town of Besa, and Skarphe,
And Augeiai; of Thronion and Tarphe,

That lie on both sides of stream Boagrios,
Known to short Ajax and Telamonios.

Ajax led forty black ships Lokrian,
Who lives across the channel Eubioa; then,
Men of the island the stanch Abantes,
Those of Eiretria and great Kalkhis,

And Histiaia, of the laden vineyard,
Alluring by the sea, the crag Dion scarp,
Those men from Styra and of Karysthos;
Where the sea wealthy resides Kerinthos.

On these, the young master Elephenor
Khalkadontiades, the prime of valor,
The chief of Abantes for commander,
Quick on their feet, hurdle nay asunder.

In long scalp locks the troops enlisted thus
Hungering body armor in their lust,
From enemies preyed by their ashen spear,
And Elephenor's forty black ships dear.

Next were the men of Athens, strong city,
A commonwealth protected in glory,
By the man Erekhtheus whom Athena,
Daughter of Zeus, cared for an Olympia.

Though he was plow, born in cornels of grain,
She placed him in her city, in her vain,
Thus her shine receives each year, bulls and rams
And the prayers of young Athenian glams.

Their commander at Troy were Peteos,
The courageous son of Menestheos,
No soldier born on earth could equal thee,
In maneuvering men and cavalry.

Save Nestor who rivaled him before time,
But by grace of age, the younger man's chime
Whist more beautifully under his name,
Where fifty Athens ships groove his fame.

Great Ajax led twelve ships from Salamis,
And beached them where Athens form them betwixt.
Then, there were those of the stronghold Argos
And the massive walls of Tirynus.

Of fortress Hermione and Asine
That lie upon the gulf; Troizen, Eionai,
The vineyard country of Epidauros,
Aigina and Mases, with their grapes to boast.

These, lord of battlecry, Diomedes,
Commanded with his comrade Sthenelos,
Whose father, the illustrious Kapaneus,
And in the third place, of Euryalos.

A figure godlike in beauty and praise,
Son of Mekisteus, Lord Talionides.
Over them ruled Diomedes, the great,
Where eighty black ships crossed strong and awaits.

In a well-built city, Mykenai,
The riches of Korinth and Kleonai,
And Orneiai and fair Araithyrea,

And Sykion; of Hyperesia and Gonoessa.

Of Sykion where Adrestos ruled on,
Pellene and the country round Aigion,
Those who held the north coast they, Aigialos,
With spacious Helike. The son of Atreus,

Agamemnon commands a hundred ships,
By far the greatest and the best! These ships
Glorying in arms and soldier's bronze horse,
With valor, the troops led their promised course.

Next, those of Lakedaimon, land of gorges,
Men who lived in Pharis, Sparta, and Messe,
Haunted by spirited doves, Bryseiai,
Of the men of fairest land of Augeiai!

Amyklai, and by the shoreline, Helos,
Of Laäs, and land around Oitylos,
These the brother of Agamemnon's par,
Menelaos led sixty ships of war.

Drawn up separately from all the rest,
Menelaos burned woods to rouse their worst,
To avenge his struggles over Helen,
And put Zeus' promises over an end.

Next came men of Arene and Pylos,
Slim towns these; Thyron over Alpheios
River, where they afford to rest awhile;
Aipy high and stony, several miles.

Kyperisseis, of bemused Pteleos,

Amphigineia, and the charming Helos;
Of Pteleos and Helos the Muses came,
Met with Thamyris the Thracian fame.

On his way from Oikhalia, thus they see
Eurytos the Oikhalian ends his spree.
These perhaps, at Dorion, better renown,
Thus because of Pride that cursed him a bone.

For, in saying he can the daughters oust,
The very Muses, outsing them, arouse,
O daughters of Zeus the winds, storm cloud bear,
They blinded him two eyes, in darkness wear.

Bereft thy voice, thy god-given songs grieved,
And stilled his harp's melodies with his lips.
The countrymen of Pylos commanded
By Nestor of Gerenia, valor-fed,

And charioteer, ninety decked ships to shore.
Then came Arkadia, of Kellene's door,
Close-order fighters around Aipytos,
At Pheneos, and of Orkhomenos.

There, many flocks. At Rhipe, at Stratie,
And the windy town of vast Enispe.
Men of Tegee and lovely Mantinae,
Men of Stymphalos and Parrhasie.

These lands were led by Agaphenor's trust,
Son of Angkhaios, sixty ships robust.
Though Arkadians able in war they thronged,
Agamemnon lend ships for them along.

That they may in dark sea pass the torment,
For knowledge they got none in this content.
So the Arkadians unto him proposed
Wise treaties that made their countries composed.

Next were men from Elis and Bouprasion
Plains confined at Olenian rock and Alesion,
By Hyrmine and land of Myrsinos.
Four captains divide, ten ships each one costs.

Thus, Epeioi embarked his old throngs,
Robust in appearance, seldom got wrongs;
Under Amphimakhos and Thalpios,
Grandsons of Aktor, sons of Kteatos

And of Eurytos. Powerful Diores
The great man of Amaryngkleides,
He commanded them – and Polyxeinos
Led division four – son of the robust

Agasthenes Augeiades. Then came
The islanders of Doulikhion's name,
And the Ekhinades, dwelt opposite
Of Elis, over the sea tides, she sits.

Meges Phyleides the captain uproar,
Begotten by the friend of Zeus, a lore,
The horseman Phyleus who moves Doulikhion
Against his father long ago. Rows on

Forty black ships to cross the Meges sea,
Such were the men with less nobility,

Except for some renowned men of the past,
Forth comes the great Odysseus and his cast.

Odysseus then, commanded the brave men
Of Kephallenia, Ithakan island;
And Neritos whose leafy heights embossed
The seawind ruffles which the seatide tossed.

Of the men of Krokyleia, of Samos
And rocky Aigilips; and Zakynthos.
These held the eastern tides of water lee,
He led them twelve ships, phantom of the sea!

His ships are painted with cheek-paint the bow,
And mighty men in its splendor they row.
Of Thoas, Andraimon's son led with pride,
Aitolian's inhabitants sans divide!

Of Pleuron, Pylene, Olenos,
Khalkis, Kalydon, rocky mountain's host,
The sons of Oineus were gone to lead,
So Thoas assumed go further instead.

The same with Meleagros, cold pale and dead,
So, forty black ships crossed the sea ahead.
Idomeneus, famed in spear-fighting,
Led the Kretans: they from Knossos warring,

Of Gortyn, town of many walls and bricks,
Of Lyktos, and its various pegs and tricks,
On Miletos and Lykastos, gleaming
White – designed by the Muses amusing.

Of Phaistos and Rhytion, pleasant brown,
All from the islands, one hundred towns,
Served under Idomeneus spearman,
Meriones, second in his command.

He fought like a slaughtering god in war,
Eighty black ships traversed the distant par.
Tlepolemos, the son of Herakles
Led nine ships from impetuous Rhodes.

In their regional division, heads thus,
Lindos, Ielysos, and bright Kameiros,
Serving under spearman Tlepolemos,
The son of wondrous Herakles endorsed.

He took his mother Astyokheia,
Who brought her out from lone Ephyra,
Out of Selleeis, wondrous river vale,
This Herakles plundered, his noble ail.

No sooner that Tlepolemos destroy
His father's uncle, old Likymnioi,
Alkmene's warrior brother; he fits out
To wander over the deep water's draught.

Suffering bitter days ahead, the odes
Are not heard, sirens nor muses erode,
But at the faint of hope, the island reach,
In every clan, beloved to Zeus, enriched.

Nireus led three great ships of Syme –
This son of Lord Khaporos majesty,
Beautifully made of all Danaäns,

After Akhilleus, first Akhaian!

Then those of Nisyros and Karpathos,
And of Kaos and the island of Kos,
Trusted in the rule of Eurypylos,
With Pheidippos and of Antiphos,

Islands of Kalydnai, ruled them thus,
A son of Herakles, sons of Thessalos
Thirty long ships in line belong the same,
With this nation's feats for lore and game.

Tell me now, Muses, that I may hear thee,
What from those great land of Argos may be,
Such that, the Argos of Pelasgians, hail,
In this long list of men my mem'ries fail!

Unto Alos, Alope, and Trekhis,
Those of Phthia, and of Hellas – I kissed
The hands of lovely women and their grace,
Beautiful men in bravery purchased.

Of the Myrmidons, and Hellenes call,
And of Akhaian, Akhilleus wall,
Led fifty ships mighty to brawl and clash
Against her turmoil or some godly slash.

But not until then, the great runner stands,
Amid the ships in desolate rage, lands,
For Breseis, his girl, soft tresses mane,
The prize he captured, fighting in his aim

Against Lyrnessos, and town of Thebes,

Overthrown by his own spearmen Myrnes
And Epistrophos, sons of Euenos
Selepiades.   For, his heart burned and tossed

For her beauty, yet lying there alone,
Knowing not, no longer the time to own,
Lingering solely in the sands of hour,
Waiting for fate to rouse his beastly scar.

Next were the men of Phylake, and those
Who held in captive, old Pyrasos,
That sweet orchard, garden of Demeter,
Thy wanting scents has reached the vivid air!

The maternal town of grazing Iton,
Beside the freshened waters of Antron,
And the bed meadows of fine Pteleos,
Under the command of Protesilaos.

Lived that intrepid fighter, fearless, bold,
But the black earth his legacies behold,
Grieving for the loss at Phylake deep,
With cheeks cut, left his bride and house adrift.

Half-finished, half-done, the hero is fine,
But the man cannot live to drink his wine,
Plunging ahead though the Dardans for Troy,
Missing their captain, spear strong an alloy.

So his troops without a leader, they choose
Podarkes, soldier son of Iphiklos,
And Phylakides, master of the sea –
Of which Podarkes, blood seed unto thee,

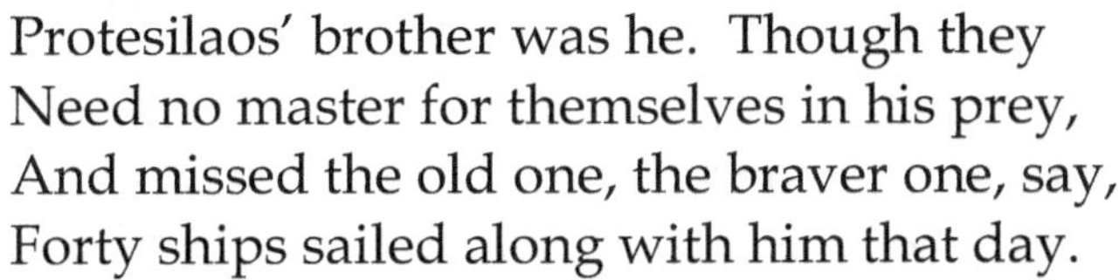

Protesilaos' brother was he. Though they
Need no master for themselves in his prey,
And missed the old one, the braver one, say,
Forty ships sailed along with him that day.

The soldiers on Pherai, the great lake,
Of Boibe and Glaphyrai, valiant-make,
In a well-kept city of Iaolkos,
Eleven ships, leagued the son of Admetos,

Eumelos, the child conceived under him
By that splendid queen Alkestis. The hymn
And glory of Pelia, old king he,
But the heaven sends him son a princely.

Next, those of Methone and Thaumakie,
Rugged Olizon and Meliboi.
Philoktetes commanded seven ships
Each with fifty oarsmen, powerful grips.

They came as expert archers to the war.
But he lay on Lemnos island, so far,
In anguish he laid there many days round,
The Akhaians marooned him there alone,

Bearing the black wound of death from a snake,
That even sages has no cure they make.
Thus, he languished there in fruitless waiting,
Until the Argives remembered, saying

To call him back. Meanwhile, his men were not
A good leader master the same, without,

Though Philoktetes missed they, Medon led –
Oileus' bastard son, by Rhene, raided.

Next, the men of Trike and Ithome,
The so-called Rocky Terraces by some,
And Oikhalia, city of Eurytos,
Over them commands great Asklepios.

Both skilled in healing, these sons of Eury',
Podaleiros and Makhaon – To sea,
Thirty decked ships were theirs for the battle,
Bending strong an arm, braving them a soul.

Then those who held the cities Gyrtone
Of Argissa, Orthe, and Elone,
And the limestones of Oloöson,
Led by a dauntless and resolute man,

Polypoites, son of Peiritoös,
He who whipped away shaggy centaurs
Of Pelion – routed them to Aithikes.
He had Leontheos, Koronos Kaineides'

Son and heir. Forty black ships to the sea!
Gouneus commanded twenty-two ships
From Kyphos. The Enienes and the brave
Peraibai under him they served,

Around Dodona wintry and northmost,
And the fertile vale of Titaressos,
Glides the lovely river to Peneios
With silver eddies and golden maelstroms.

The home of a Styx riding as it sworn,
The lovely whirlpool that salutes its born,
Unto lores of the old, and stories gain
High dreamers reach, in the hands of it, chain.

The Magnetes were led by Protoös,
The son of Tenthredon, by Peneios
They lived mount Peleion' shimmering sides,
Forty black ships had for Trojan ides.

These were the lords and captains of the sea,
Of Danaän's farer hailed and highly,
But tell, Muses, of all men and horses,
Who were to Agamemnon's the finest?

As for the battle horses, whining brave,
Of Pheres' pastures skilled the stalwart fave,
And Eumelos who breeds the most in share,
As fleet of birds, matching colors and fair,

And level of the hair in its crupper,
In age that ties their beloved master.
Apollo, methought breeds them at his stead,
Fearsome in the eyes of the exquisite mead.

Of all fighting men, most formidable,
Ajax Telamonios, stout and able,
That is, while Akhilleus raged apart,
He towered them all with his soul and heart.

So all the stallions who are drawn to war,
And all the charioteers, their speed and car,
But now, lo! Hoe desperate to see him,

Raging over the king, lay alone slim.

And his people, marshalled the breaking waves,
Played the discus to kill time, and, on shaves,
The sands with javelin to sport their bore,
Waiting Akhilleus' signal to war.

Meanwhile their teams, beside the chariots, tore,
And champed at clover and parsley for sore,
Their war-cars shrouded in the shades of rest,
Shelters the moment till his rage behest.

And, longing for their chief, beloved thee,
Idly waiting to fit their anxious flee,
Throughout the camp, drifted in calumny,
Taking no part in that day's fighting wee.

Yet the host devoured the plain, marching strong,
As if the prairie is in fire, along,
The ground beneath it rumbled like a quake,
As when Zeus the lord of lightning bolts make.

Anger, resentment aginst Typhoeus
Lashing the earth around Einarimos!
Where his couch is said to rest in its leaves,
The groans of anger in keenness of whips.

So thunderously grumbled earth and wet,
Under the trampling of their marching feet,
Consuming like fire the open meadow,
Under one robust fright of their shadow!

Iris arrived Troy, running on the wind,

As messenger of Zeus for Trojans keen,
Bearing news of grim and forbidding grey,
Like stormcloud of the god, to Trojans pay.

Assembled the army – both old and young,
At the gates of Priam, high walls, its fang,
When she came near, stood in front of them, say Her
voice unto Polites' likeness pray.

The first eye to measure the Argives foes,
Sprinting unto the field, touched the bellows
Of their hearts, until; In his guise, she stand
At the burial smooth, of Aisyetes' mound.

Waiting there to see the Akhaians leave
Their camps and ships, Then, in his soul bereaved,
What might happen must be the will of man,
What god content themselves, we'll understand.

To Priam, Iris spoke: "Sir, king Priam,
Will thou indulge thyself to talk on sum
In a way inordinate as for peace,
When time has lost the measure on your knees?

The truth is there: vanguards of rashing flair,
War is upon us! This, the smell of air!
Many times I've come a hand in combat,
But never have I seen a foe like that!

In such array, marching on like fire and hale,
Committed, every man, drunken ale!
The grasses are burned, the meadow is dust,
As grains of sands forwarding; but, we must!

Hektor, thou art the one I call upon,
Shall I direct thee, now, take an action,
That crowd is of various tongues and kinsmen,
Receiving instruction from their captains,

Sort them off, divide their gathering harsh,
And this army shall in confusion bashed!"
So Hektor punctiliously obey her,
The goddess Iris, reserved on their care.

Then he dismissed the army assembled,
To gather their effects and arms. Gambled
No second to waste a bit in this hour,
Where a true Trojan should be a warrior!

All city gates wide, wide open and roar,
Yawned out the soldiers, mighty as a boar!
And the units poured out, in perfect line,
The chariots and horses, tremendous whine.

Come, our equipped soldiers of Troy at hand,
Young and old to defend their precious land,
Wail in confidence, usual Trojan smart,
No battle for a thousand year to chart.

In ready positions, the archers reach
To skyward bulge in their synchronized teach.
Walls high to pronounce the victory's wit,
And count the skulls their offenders submit!

Rising in isolation, on the plain
Facing the walled city, a ridge attain,

A bluff, plain-spoken to all sides, forethought
A strategic spot, one day shall support.

Here, at Briar Hill, both men and gods, knew,
Where the Amazon named Myrine lieu,
On the tomb, they anchored their primal smut
Against the enemy's unwitting plot.

So the Trojans and allies waiting proves
Formed the battle, as nearby mountain moves,
But tall, with helmet flashing in their eyes,
Hektor the valiant-hearted soldier cries!

The great son of Priam Trojans he led,
Chief of all divisions gaining ahead,
In power and best, the hefted spear swift,
Hoist in the treble breath of eagerness lift.

The Dardans to Aineias warring keep,
Splendid Aphrodite herself thus conceived,
Under Ankhises, the vales of Ida,
In a man's embrace, lying immortal!

His inferior named sons of Antenor,
Both battle-wise, Akamas and Arkhelokos!
Then those from Zeleia, the lower slope,
Unto Ida's waters, dark and still grove.

Serving under, Lykaon's shining son,
Pandaros, Apollo taught in the sun,
To use the bow in a golden errand
And hint the spot that his victor has won.

Adresteia's men, on the hinterland
Of Apaisos, Pityeia, crag of sand,
Unto Treria. All these were led by
Adrestos, captain honored and mighty.

He led with Amphios of linen dress,
Both sons of Merops Perkosios no less,
The seer profoundest of all seers is he,
Who told them to refuse the smitten key.

But they refused his words, heedless headstrong,
Driven onward by dark powers along,
Of death the sirens, and the Muses knew,
The seer the same, they decline his view.

And then those who live around Sestos,
At Praktion, Perkote, and Abydos,
And old Arisbe. Their captain Asios,
Whose name is Hyrtakides, who amused

The sorrel horses to Seleen south.
Hippothoös, led the Pelasgians tough,
From Larisa's rich plowland he is trained,
With Pylaios, sons of the Pelagian

Lethos Teutamides. Then, Thracians great
From beyond the seaward vales and the strait,
From Helle's rushing waters are bounded,
Through Akamas and Peiroös, they are led.

Sons of Troizenos Keades, Euphemos
Led the Kikones of the distant shores,
And those distant archers, Paiones called,

And Pyraikhmes led from Amydon old.

From Axios bemirroring the whole plain,
And many other sons in various gain.
Pylaimenes the Paphlagonians detailed,
Shaggy, great-hearted, and disheveled.

From the wild mule country Enetoi,
Men who held lofty Erythenoi,
On Kytoros and lordly Sesamos,
Who had their homes near at Parthenios.

Of Kromma, and the land called Aigialos.
Thus, captains Odios and Epistrophos
Led the Halizones from Alybe,
Far eastward, where silver gorges are plenty.

The Mysians Khromis led, with Ennomos,
Reader of birdflight. Signs of flurring dross
Yet golden veil to his ivory skill,
To Akhilleus' bath his name's a kill.

Not from his scribes of feather he may sing,
Nor fly from the death blows he might bring,
But battering hands, Peleus' son achieved,
The greatest runner shall one day receive.

Phrygians under Phorkys and Askanios,
From distant Askante, fighters utmost,
The Lydians and Meiones, leaders had
Mesthles and Antiphos, ready and mad.

These were sons born by Gigaie lake to

Talaimenes. They led men under brow
In the mountains of Tmolos,
Nastes commanded Karians and its host,

In their own tongue, the master breeds them poise,
On men of Phthiron, men of Miletos,
Peaks of Mykale, rills of Maiandros
Led by Nastes and Amphimakhos!

Wearing gold, blithe as a girl, he had gone
To war with his men. But gold cannot stand
The fool of war, when AKhilleus thrust
His sword, to spoil the earthen and it lust.

Akhilleus Aiakides would frown
And he and his gold shall together drown.
Sarpedon led Lykians with Glaukos,
From Lykie afar, from whirling Xanthos!*

Book III
BEAUTIFUL HELEN

Officers flanked the Trojan squadron square,
Drew up the border like claws of a bear,
Fringed the walls of Troy in prudent bellow,
The screech of wild din of arms and marrow.

Sortied well the officers and outrank,
Clamorous lines before the Trojan hank,
Facing the heavens, beating away storm
And winter's misery, flaying the norm.

Over Ocean's stream, the flaying of fate,
Thrashing, the darkness, and lashing the hate,
The call to decay each bravery's aim,
Slaughter the pygmy warriors they proclaim!

Cranes of the dawn descending in the east,
Beaked of cruel attack, hoarse of a beast!
Encroach the fearless, in courage resort,
Both noble plan, the eminent has worth.

The Akhaians for their part came on still,
Raging over their breath, the dowse they feel,
Shoulder to shoulder sworn the drench ahead,
Holding their fury struck a wimping dead.
Imagine the mist the south wind roll on hills,
A blowing curse for sheperds, bothered chills,
But for thieves, better than a night fall be,

Where early the eyes surmise memory.

Mist where a man can see a stone-throw far,
Not anymore, for thick the Argives spar,
So dense the dust that clouded covering,
Devouring the plain, strongly advancing.

And near, and nearer, the front ranks approach,
Until one affront the Akhaian notch,
Detaching himself first in the battle,
The Trojans pauses with their wild rattle.

Vivid and beautiful, Alexandros,
Wearing a cowl of leopard skin and bows
Hang on his back, a longsword on his hips,
Gallant words feat on his kissable lips!

With two spears capped in pointed bronze, he had,
Slices of carrion in the war-bath mad,
He shook the dust on his noble advent,
And called out the best the Argive appends.

To meet with him a fracas, face to face,
Thus, Menelaos, watch the figure brace,
With long strides in the clearness of the day,
Knew him and thrilled with joy, he firmly sway.

A ravenous lion, before his name,
Hungry in the tissues of heavy game,
Say to an antlered deer, or a wild goat,
Shall rend the bones and feast the bloody dote.

Though hunters around him assail him prey,

Keep the klutz in his fool, a seer-fast way,
So Menelaos thrilled when he beheld,
Alexandros before his eyes, he said:

"I'll cut him morsel, adulterous mongrel!"
Thus, he vaulted down his car, wraths compel
Him, gather all his gear toward the guy,
Menelaos shaven in fright to die.

But when Alexandros caught sight of this man,
Emerging from the ranks, he understand,
His heart misgave, the fact in his soul lacks
One more step of nerve to express his lax.

And he recoiled to his companions, say,
Not to incur the deadly clash he may,
Retreated thus, the augur in his face,
The clouds in hiding, the light of disgrace.

A man who stumbles upon a viper
In a mountain glen whose soul a shutter,
Jump aside, and run the fastest recluse,
Tremble upon trembles, the sly-fast loosed.

Whereas, shuddering knees he had a quake,
Tremor in his veins, a drought in the lake,
Pallor in his cheeks, insult in his name,
Alexandros move away right, ashamed.

He backs and backs away, the army deep,
In the same way, paced backward, in their sleeves,
Into the Trojan lines and edged their thick,
Dreading the son of Atreus frolic.

Hektor watched his brother, and said in scorn:
"You bad-luck charm, Paris, courage I warn!
The great lover! The gallant sight! Take heed,
Thou shall die unmarried, without a seed!

Would to god you had! Better this way be
Than dishonor your Troy so cowardly!
Now, they can laugh, Akhaians, bravery,
Who thought thou art a first rate soldiery!

A champion, going by looks! Go on, flirt!
Thou hast no backbone, powerless as grit!
How gallant you stand there, shouting hero,
Yet there's no staying power in your claw!

Were you this way then, with your crews and ale,
When you cross the sea and entreat a tale?
When you brought home a lovely woman here
From a far land, of distant virtue and seer?

That girl, already married, she had been,
Brother-in-law, and husband juts indeed?
Great soldiers are they! Great warrior and king!
Puts enmity between our nations string?

Such a ruin to your father and his
Realm, your actions cost, nothingness hiss'd!
Joy for our enemies and shame for you!
Now, can you move for Menelaos too?

You'll find out what a fighting man is he,
Whose flower-like wife you hold but tightly,

No charm would come from Muses or a harp,
Or Aphrodite's favor in your strap…
Ah the clean-limbed body and flowing hair,
Nay these shall perish lurked in your affair,
When you lay down to make love to the dust!
What slaves these Trojans are, but in your lust!

If not, long since you might have worn the stones
For all the wrongs you have drawn in the throne!"
The beautiful prince, Alexandros, said:
"Ah, Hektor, harsh words are kept by the dead.

Harshness is more than just, when heart arash,
Remember though your spirit made and wash'd
In the ax-edge whetted sharpness it shines,
Through timbers, through pillows, through soul
enshrines.

Thy ax triple in power, hewing out
A beam for the shipwright, just not without;
That is the way the breast encased your heart,
An ax and a heart, drench vivid and smart.

My own gifts from pale-gold Aphrodite,
Taunts not me like the same. But in beauty
Of a man, a princely light in my face,
Clothed in flawless lovelies and youthful grace.

Glorious things the gods bestow should not pest
One's person; more so, despised and detest,
May it be so as the gods will to us,
Wishing may not bring them, in smell or ash.

Now, if fighting is what you want from me,
Make all them Trojans and Akhaians see,
Down their arms and shield, arrows and skilled
spear,
Let Menelaos and me alone adhere.

Between our lines, in single combat hold
A duel for Helen and the Spartan gold!
Whoever gets the upper hand in this,
Shall take the treasure and woman in peace.

Let the rest part as friend, let all take oath,
And live in our rich land, in this I haught,
Before you make sail for Argos abode,
The land of lovely womankind and boats!"

Hektor's heart lightened-up, from hearing him,
The dull roughness sheds as clouds smooth it slim,
And down the Trojan center, with his lance,
Held mid-haft, he drove, calling: "Battalions,

Halt!" Till he brought them to a stand-at-ease.
The long-haired Akhaian soldiers appease
Their bows and arrows, spearheads on the dust,
The stones and fire-wick, culls the outrage passed.

But high and clear, they heard them shouts their king,
Agamemnon: "Hold on, Argives! Don't bring
Your blows of death thereto. Hektor, flashing
In that helmet, his proclamation sing!"

Archers lowered their bows, and fell silent,
The whole land and the sky above their tent,

As Hektor to both enemies appeal:
"Hear me Trojans, Akhaians, as you will.

Hear the proposals of Alexandros,
Because of whom this whole matter endorsed,
He asks all other Trojans and other
Akhaian soldiers put their arms under.

In the ground shall they stay for the meantime
While he and Menelaos fight between the lines,
For Helen and the Spartan gold shall be,
Take the treasure and woman home with thee.

The rest, with solemn oaths, part as comrades."
Hushed were the armies both, face and the ends,
Across the field, while king Menelaos,
Clarion of war, address to them: "Of those

Ears, listen too to thee, as the iron
Enters my sleeves, deepest in my carrion,
Yet I agree, the Trojans and Argives
Should withdrew in peace and in amities.

You have borne so much hardship in this squabble,
A tiff I must end, a spat I should troll,
Whom Alexandros began. So old Death
To him for whom the hour it takes whose breath!

The rest of you, part peacefully, and soon,
This, augury no man may choose a spoon,
But bring down a black ewe, and snow-white ram,
For the earth and Helios a good ransom.

Reckless seeds, and unworthy sons they had,
But no man's overweening his soul clad,
Pompous against Zeus, age has various mind,
But the youth is changeable, lest he's blind.

To look before and after, clearly notes,
The beauty and the ugly as one loathes,
That he shall see the best for his own soul,
And measure the good interest for all!"

At this, all hearts are lifted by his words,
To end the war, both sides with their warlords,
And backing chariots into line, stepped out
The men, and disarmed their weapons about.

Heaped at close intervals affirms the ground,
Hektor sent two runners perfectly sound
To bring a sheep, and summon Lord Priam.
Agamemnon dispatched, at the same time,

Talthybios to the ships, bidding him
A sheep as well, and he obeyed and bring.
In the lax of time, two warring walls stand,
Would blood or water wash the Trojan sand?

Now, to Helen made, Iris on her way,
Appears as Laodike, sister-in-ley,
Loveliest of Priam's daughter, and wife
Of Helikaon, on Antenor's life.

Found her weaving, bound in the violets,
Stuff that she made, for arms and corsets,
Iris approaches her, and swiftly said:

"Come, dearest! Come outside! Big changes wade.

See how Trojans and Akhaians at ease,
They made war, weeping to death, in the least,
Unending in the cruel plain and glen,
But no, not right now! The warcry has end!

Their shields were rested, their spears entrusted,
The grounds are hollows, and the rage is dead!
It seems Alexandros and the great king
Menelaos in single-combat bring.

With battle spears for you! O Helen dear,
The man who shall win, wins thee, blood and tears!"
Well as the goddess, golden tongue bespoke,
Infused in thyme and cinnamon soak.

In Helen's heart lurks smoky sweetness puffed,
And marjoram desire but rare and soft,
For the man who took her first as a bride,
And for her parents, and her ancient pride.

Quickly she soaked herself, silvery veil,
As her tears in the crystals of her tale,
Made her way to the chamber left astride,
Yet not without a comfort, brood her side.

As a princess she, two maids in waiting,
Ready to fix her morose and clinging,
Her name, daughter of Pittheus, Aithre,
And lady wide-eye known as Klymene.

Soon these women, at the Skaian Gates tour,

Where king Priam and his high counselors
Were sitting – Thymoites, Panthoös,
The honorable Lampos, Klytios,

With the soldier known as Hiketaon,
Clear-mind Antenor and Oukalegon.
Peers in his domain, yet of age refined
And strengthless at war, but strong will confined.

Perching in the towers, their voice rung,
Like shrill cicadas in a summer hung,
And fathom bass in a long rhythmic ode,
So droned and murmured these old wisemen lord.

On the tower, watching as Helen climb
The stairs, approaching them, in ebbing rhyme:
"We cannot rage at her, wonder it not,
How a Trojan or an Akhaian spot,

Should for long, suffer the perils of war
Because of this… man, all night wished his star."
"Unearthliness, fairly high a goddess,
A woman to look at, 'bove all the rest!"

"Ah, but still, even so, in all her grace,
Should verve to thy ships, and go back her place,
That this scourge went away in our children
And wife. Unlucky portent needs to end."

Voices were to Helen's ear, Priam called:
"Come here, dear child, sit here beside me. Hold
Not to blame a god for bringing this woe
Against the Akhaians, for our sorrow.

Come, tell me who the big man is out there,
Sleeved in a powerful figure he bear,
Other men are taller, but never I saw
A soldier clean-cut as he, I should know

His royal bearing, kingly man was he?"
Reply thus Helen, in her great beauty,
"Revere you as I do, I dread you too,
Dear father. Painful death should bear me too,

And sweeter it embraces my heart's hush,
On the day I joined your son, by that lush,
And left the pillows and bridal chamber,
My grown lilies, and roses, how I dare?

But nay, no death came to me, in my wept,
Long as I ever pined on, the god has left.
Regarding your question, I should answer,
That man is Agamemnon, commander

And lord of the plain of Argos, far-land,
The son of Atreus, our king at hand,
Formidable soldier, and battle brand,
Mighty brother to my wanton husband.

Or was that life a dream?" The old man gazed,
And mused on her, softly cried: "Thy amaze!
O fortunate son of great Atreus,
Child of destiny, happy soul is loosed!

How many sons of Akhaia serve you?
Into the vineyard country of Phrygia,

The host of nimble ponies, as they say,
Otreus and Mydon's people, I pray!

In those days, encamped at the Sangrios,
A river we used to drink. And obvious
As an ally would allot me my place
When the Amazons came down in haste.

Those women who were fighting men and death,
But thy host never equal this on earth,
The army of the keen-eyed men of fate,
The Akhaian army roving my state."

Still gazing out, he made a sight of awe
Unto Odysseus height, the old man draw:
"Tell me, my child, who that officer be,
Valiant and bravery in looks was he.

The son of Atreus stands a head taller,
But this warlord appears a chest deeper,
His shoulders broader by the length of it,
His gear lies on the ground, and full-bodied.

Still he goes like bellwether, to and fro,
And up and down, the rank and file he go',
A ram I'd call him, burly, think with fleece,
Keeps a flock of silvery sheep and beast."

Helen shaped by heaven answered the king:
"That's Laertes' son, Odysseus, my king,
The great tactician he was called to us,
Bred in Ithaka, in all ways of wars."

Antenor, the alert man, interposed:
"My lady, there indeed, you knockout it close!
A hint to our passion, this man could be,
But as stars made route, they are here with thee.

Once, long ago, he came here, Odysseus,
Entreat with your husband Menelaos,
As guests they shovel the gold ores we please,
And become friends – brothers in arms and wits.

From him, learned characters and stratagem,
A man must possess before a harem.
Among us, Trojans, in our feast your spouse,
Broad in shoulder as him, just and likewise.

Seated yet overtopped him in height, dear,
And Odysseus looked ahead kinglier,
When each of them stood up to make a plea,
An argument before us all alacrity.

But Menelaos said few words rather
Headlong, succinct, but clearly: Commoner
Thy words, not vague, not long-winding, to bard,
And younger was he of the two, is that?

Then, in his turn, the tactician rose, stood,
Looked to the ground, playing his lowly brood,
Forward and backward the staff he held moves,
Few bird chirps passed, and he stomp his hooves!

First, obstinate he must, his acts imposed,
And slow of wit, his eyes rolling over its dross,
Gripping his staff, aye, you would say abrupt,

The surly fellow stands an empty tat.

Yet, and yet, as he launched his voice aloud,
Breathe out the strong bellow in his chest, sound
Of trumpets and flutes, the Muses disguised,
But he himself speaking, not for the gods!

The wind in his words, drove the snowflakes out,
Thick and fast as the winter of the South!
Then Odysseus, no mortal rival him,
The wonders of the Muses is with him!

The look of him no longer made us frown,
That the mortal is a gift from Zeus' throne!"
The third figure he saw, the old man asked:
"Who is that other one, if I may ask,

So massive a wall, strongly-built is he,
Towering heads and shoulders, who is he
Stands above the Argive troops?   So Helen
Tall in her gown, and silver cloak, she rend:

"The giant soldier – Ajax, is his name,
The rugged sea wall, the Akhaian fame!
Opposite him, among the Kretans stay,
Is lanky Idomeneus, I say.

With captains around him, in lofty pride,
Menelaos, whom wargod Ares side,
Receives him often in our Spartan house,
When he traversed over the Kretan bowls.

I see all the Akhaian now, my lord,

Whom I might reckon, in spear and in sword,
Names I might know; except for two I scarce,
The captains Kastor, breaker of horses,

And the boxer Polydeukes, my lord,
These are my brothers, mother bore them both.
Were these not in the fleet I might amiss,
At Lakedaimon, where my orchard hiss'd?

Or did they cross in the long ships without,
Refrain from entering the war, I doubt,
Because I dread vie stranded talk of me,
And curses on my head, exceedingly?"

So Helen wondered about her sight long,
But her brothers lay motionless along
The arms of life-bestowing earth beneath,
At Lakedaimon, of their fathers stead.

Meanwhile, by lane and walls the criers plain,
The sacred sheep and bearing wine unstain'd,
That warms the heart, the gift of vineyard ground,
A goatskin ponderous, yielding befound.

And one, Idaios, carrying the gold –
Golden goblets and winebowl , thus behold,
Shining and shimmering luster and light,
Reached for the aged king, called him a-bright:

"Son of Laomedon, rise to your feet!
Master soldiers of both army, indeed,
Trojan breaker of horses, lauds be raised,
Akhaian mailed in bronze, thy honor brazed.

Request that you be present in the plain,
For peace offerings and oath here domain,
Here, Alexandros of the Trojan hub
And Menelaos, the wargod beloved,

Shall fight with battle spears over Helen,
She and the treasure to him commends,
To thee who wins the battle, arm araised,
As for the rest, by solemn pact is placed,

Thereafter in this rich land pace shall dwell,
While they return to the grazing land swell
Of Argos and to Akhaia, attest,
Home of fair women, this battle commence."

At this announcement, by the crier, spook
A tremor the old king, head to foot, shook,
He said: "Harness the team." Hastily done,
There is no stop to a fate still unknown.

Stepping in his chariot, Lord Priam took,
The wheeling reins, and leaning back, he look,
Tugging the horses until Antenor
Mounted, in cheerless face, on his favor.

Out of the plain, from the Skaian Gates, drove,
Swift the chariots headed toward the grove,
Reined in within the battle line, they cease,
In an open ground, once a pasture breeze.

Between the Trojan and Akhaian arm,
Agamemnon and Odysseus alarm,

Rose from the thick grass of braving soldier,
At the pact, submitting one another.

The criers, noble retainers brought forth
The sacrificial sheep, votive they worth,
Prepared the bowls of wine, and rinse the hands
Of the commanders of peace-seeking lands!

Then the son of Atreus drew from his hips,
The sheath knife handing, hinted bladefast snips,
Along his longsword scabbard, golden keep,
The pact is sacred, while the blade is deep.

From the brows of ram and ewe he cut thrust,
The soft fleece into soul, breathless passed,
Then round the knife the officers derived,
Pass the solemn rites, with arms open wide!

Agamemnon pray in the name of all:
"O Father Zeus, Power over Ida!
Greatest, most glorious thy name exhibit,
Profoundest heaven, in thy hands and wit.

O Helios! By whom all things are perceived,
And sentiments overheard! Hear we plead!
O rivers! O black earth! And hails below!
Chastisers of men dead so long ago!

Unto this solemn vow, we carry on,
Be witness all: preserve this pact we s my worn,
If, Alexandros would kill Menelaos,
Then, he should keep Helen fair for this cost,

And the gold, thou shall bring in his chamber,
While we sail homeward, these Argives dreamer!
But if Alexandros be killed, forlorn,
The Trojans should surrender Helen sworn,

And the treasure they must pay tribute due,
From now on, and to their descendants too.
Thus, Priam and his sons to this refuse,
Though his son be killed, shall my weapon use

Until it tires me to take back the win,
Or until when I say the war should grin!"
The pitiless bronze knife, edged in hard cross
The gullets of the rite, and laid it browse

The quivering ground, beneath utter death,
The ebbing of breath, breathe farewell to earth!
Dip thus the wine up, into aurum lay,
The captains tipped this offerings and pray.

To the gods who never die, prayers rise,
Here is the way their supplication cries:
"O Zeus, almighty and most gracious god!
You, who does in immortality trod!

Let any parties this oath is break fell,
Calamitously rake brains off as well,
Decanted as this wine drops on the ground,
They and their children, their honors in mound,

Let their wives suffer the indolent ease,
For making the oath their husbands dismissed."
This the oath ran but Zeus would not abide,

What they swore is not the best heaven side.

Now Dardan Priam, king of Trojan fair,
Spoke to the assembly this way: "One air
We breathe today, O warriors east and west,
Trojans and Akhaians one word I crest.

Shall I go back to the town Illion,
Windy enough for a wobbly lion,
For, I cannot bear to watch my son fight
Against Menelaos with all his might.

A man whom a wargod stands on his back,
Cheering strength and strength, armoring his rack,
I doubt not Zeus knew the end of all these,
All the gods know which of the two shall bliss."

Placed he the carcasses fresh before him,
The ram and the ewe in his chariot trimmed,
Then he stepped aboard the majestic wheels,
Holding the horses, while Antenor stills

The royal car, the faint in his tears jeer,
Then circling the altar rite, in the leer,
Drove toward Illion, the windy ground,
The father, in grimace, awaits the sound.

Then Hektor the prince and Odysseus back,
Paced off the dueling ground, In this act,
Two tokens in gilded bronze helm beheft,
Tossing the stars, the air moves right and left.

Which man would cast his weapon the first,

Far away the winding chariot rehearsed,
Alexandros and Menelaos aflame,
Both the armies pray to the god the same:

"O mighty Zeus, Ida's power supply!
May he who brought this sylvan trouble die!
Let him laid waste in the dark undergloom,
As for ourselves, comrades of peace we bloom."

"This battle, may it end the nearest, now,
O mighty splendor, kill its troublous vow!
Let the girl and gold begotten thy hour
In sweet pomegranate and cheesy sour!"

"O gods of Olympos give us the boon,
This fateful craving shall in blood aswoon,
Let peace come right, like thunder on its way,
Sweet homeward with our wives, and children play!"

"Whoever's led to the pitfall of grime,
Despicable sword in his hands and crime!
May we end this trouble, for girl instead,
And on our own girl, encompass ahead!"

Time had come, and the prince buckled his mail,
Prince Alexandros, Helen's consort, hail,
His armor of silver and golden plate,
A chest that bears the cuirass of his fate!

Molded were the shins, silver circlets good,
Around his chest the symbol of his brood,
Lykaon his brother whose chest befits,
This handsome prince soul, in his duel meets.

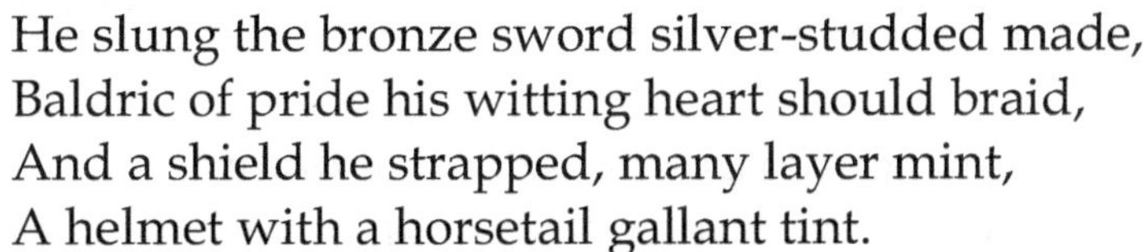

He slung the bronze sword silver-studded made,
Baldric of pride his witting heart should braid,
And a shield he strapped, many layer mint,
A helmet with a horsetail gallant tint.

On that head, a plume of gracious temple,
Breaking his sweat to an oil-scented fall,
A solid spear he took, a hand grip fast,
Waving crest of valor the Trojan clashed.

Meanwhile, the great soldier Menelaos,
His own equipment he worn and embossed,
Chest of a bear, strength of an oxen paw,
An eclipse to the shining face of 'now'.

Armed in splendor, in each army apart,
Waits for the moment the bloodbath may start,
On the Trojan side, prince Alexandros,
With the Akhaian, king Menelaos!

Each glaring scornfully foe and foe,
The excitement of all has tend the show
Of valiance and rage for a prize to won,
Beautiful Helen, watching in the sun.

Fierce were the delight, the heart stomping wild,
Horse-breaking Trojan and leg-armored child
Of war! The moment is clear as the sun,
Cheers to Helen and her blood-champion men!

Alexandros opened the air he hurled
The long-shadowing spear a rashfast earned,

Atreides fair on the round shield poised up,
There is nothing these two may ever stop.

He struck the armor hard, though it fell damp,
The impact bent the air a madding pomp,
The second he cast and rouse his bronze spear,
Against Atreus' son, with little cheer.

Menelaos opened his mouth to pray,
To Father Zeus, he wanton beg this way:
"O Zeus, make the first man pay lofty pain
Who made these troubles. In Death be him chain!

Let his humble knees on my hands implore,
The sullen guilt in my soul slumber wore,
That the hearts of those who live after us,
May know what love he made, yet he is dust!"

He aims at the prince, and the hoist is oft,
Hurled his spear forward, and hitting aloft,
To hit his adversary 'gainst the shield,
His first strike awed the soldiers in the field!

With speed challenging the younger rival,
The spear went through the polished hide, the soul
Of Paris might have been impart, but through
The heavy cuirass it ripped, as it flew.

The shirt is cut, yet the flesh is secured,
The young prince escaped its lethal poured.
Paris, twisting in his right, pass it flaw,
Eluding but death in that certain blow!

Veteran of wars, losing not his outrage,
Draw his longsword out to manacle fate,
Lord Menelaos reared and struck on him
Failed in a helmet ridge his longsword bring!

Lifting his eyes on heaven, he groaned thus:
"O Father Zeus, all of the gods, I pass
Mine words against your cruel acts on me,
A hopeful man I was, yet you listened wee!

I thought to make Alexandros to pay
The crime against me! But what luck you may?
Thy grip is softened, my spear is in vain,
And missed him twice, shattering me insane!"

Angry more than ever, the bear persists,
His heart's atrocity, his fate consists,
Abound in anger, he laid hold and spun
The foe prince toward the line Akhaian.

Chocked by the chin strap, swift thus and close,
Into his throat the spear again has lost,
For a well-stitched band covered that blood thrust,
And beneath his helmet, courage, alas.

Menelaos' name, his own glory rose,
Well in fact, the man would pull him close,
Thus the spear would thrust in him directly,
Had he not pulled by fair Aphrodite!

That goddess perceives, with her clear eyes, see,
The restless knock of Paris shrouding flee,
She snapped the band of oxhide, blurring see,

But the beast waked his anger fervently.

Now heave and helmet swayed on his head,
He whirled it round, and round, threw it dead,
Unto the Akhaian his helmet flee,
And his own people had caught it for thee.

And once again, the third time, to him kill,
He lunged a deep breath, aim his lance at will,
But away does Alexandros escaped
As swift as a god, gotten off his rave.

Aphrodite hides him in the cold mist,
Took Alexandros off the battling beast!
In his chamber, his own fragrant bed,
Went him mute the instance of death ahead.

He stayed there, waiting, while the goddess went
To summon Helen, lady fair and scent.
She went in the chamber with ladies throng,
Off the barricade, these firebrands along.

Then, Aphrodite plucked one of her gowns,
Resemble a lady who once made her soft spuns,
A spinning-woman for her parade and pomp,
Back at Lakedaimon, her home, her fond.

In this guide, Aphrodite spoke to her:
"Come home with me, Alexandros is there,
Invites your pleasantry, this man asks,
On the ivory-laid bed your presence asked.

On your own bedchamber he lies at ease,

Waiting for your coming, your hugs and kiss,
Freshly dressed he was, fresh as dewdrops are,
So handsome he was, though he's gone from war!

Could you imagine he just came from clash?
But nay, one may say he's graced a dance, wash'd
In the waters of youthfulness he laid,
In the sweet resting pillows of your bed."

Aphrodite, the goddess of beauty,
Described him to her, this much vanity,
While Helen's heart beats faster in her breast,
A taste of honey dew in Paris' quest.

Quick were the rhythm, from beating within,
Her senses are felt, pulses never thin,
In the guise of a woman, she's hiding,
The flawless throat of her, thus seducing.

Helen called her by her name, pronouncing:
"O immortal madness, goddess I sing,
Why make me crave for a man handsomely?
Should I fall again and again to thee?

Unto Phrygian walls, my witness shall home,
Eastward, and eastward more, to thy kingdom!
Or unto Moienie, if friends are found,
Since Menelaos deserved my hand?

All your cunning ways I found dimly cast,
If you want Alexandros' constant lust,
Then serve in my place, and be my disguise!
I shall be unworthy of your despise.

Leave the bright path then, the gods over me,
And walk no more about the heavenly!
Unhappy for him, shield him, till at last,
He marries your graces, or enslave your trust.

I would not join Paris his fragrant bed,
Abasement in my name is strongly made,
I cannot make him luxurious when I
Made someone's chamber bed, a curse to die.

Whispering, there should be many around,
And among Trojan women shall abound,
As though my pain is not enough to bear,
For I have been pleasing but another!"

Says goddess Aphrodite: "Better not
Grim on my part, vexing my name this plot,
Then you, shall I hate, as I cherished thee,
A curse shall I enfold in you highly.

More so, do you think I have less than can
Make you more than sorrow and taciturn?
That Trojans and Danaäns anger grew,
Of these your bad ends, the stake is on you!"

Now, afraid of the goddess, Helen fair
Enfolds the goddess' shining robe silver,
She turned to go, without a say; of course
The goddess guides her outside the wide doors.

Yet unseen by the mortal attendants,
Guided by the goddess, ahead she stands

In the goddess' delight, thy heart is stuck,
Helen and Paris, to the goddess' luck!

Unto Alexandro's brilliant house, she trod,
Maids quickly work, to honor the god,
Mounting her to the high chamber of love,
Aphrodite, who smiles on smiling love,

Brought a chair to her ease, facing down the man,
Helen, daughter of Zeus, greeted :
"Home from the war, you should have perish there,
And be brought down by that beast, great soldier!

Why don't you challenge him again, Paris,
Just like what you do, what to do, at least,
Are you a better man – you used to say,
More skilful yet, the hands becoming grey.

But, shall I go or not, my virtue stands,
Promise: do not go to war; or speak 'gans,
The rash of fools are many, crumbled in the sand,
The land is a nail pierced against the hand.

Says Paris: "Bitter not, my love, to thee,
But kindness rule between us, truthfully,
It is true that he won, over my joy,
Under Athena's shield, mustered and toyed,

Next time, I may. Next time, I shall victor,
We, too have gods as our protector!
Right now, O desert dove, let's drop the war,
And give ourselves the pleasure of the star!

My soul longs the hour, so possessed by you,
Not even at Lakedaimon, by the view,
When I took you off the shores, sailed away,
My heart's content fondled, O night and day!

Remember when I first make love, adieu,
At Krannae Island, sure, I have loved you!
But now, greater desire lifted my soul,
You, dearest love, my witness in this hall!

Thus went him softly fragrant pillow throw,
And she followed the winds where it flow,
Making flowers bloom in the desert sing,
Waters flow in the timid of a spring!

Time has no meaning, forever is true,
In the ivory-ladden bed, lovers knew,
While Menelaos roamed outside to find,
Like a wild beast, hunting the prince divine!

Godlike Alexandros, in the mist hides,
Pleasant pillows, Aphrodite provides.
But not a Trojan, not one allies could
Produce Paris, it seems though they were fooled.

Thus Agamemnon, the Lord Marshall says:
"O Trojans, Dardans, allies, and comrades,
Beyond question, Menelaos has won,
Therefore, Helen of Argos, for this man!

And the gold to be surrendered at hand,
Thou shall pay tribute to the Akhaian!
Thus, compensate this virtue to the sun,

Your generation and the next should grant!"

To this judgment of king Agamemnon,
The pact has to be done, the sacred plan,
To Trojans heart, the payment burns their wall,
But assent the Akhaians, after all."*

Book IV
The Arrow

At high Olympos, mountain golden-floored,
Seats of power, the gods hailed and adored,
The gods seated – Zeus and his council all,
Gracious Hebe served nectar in the hall.

With cups of gold, a comfort to their lips,
Wine ambrosia, the soft water it keeps,
Run through the toast, as one another's cheers,
Looking down Illion, threshold of tears!

Tersely, Zeus intend to ruffle Hera,
With oblique words, yet hiding enigma,
In a cutting tone, the god remarked, thus,
The council followed his diversions must:

"Two goddesses took Menelaos' pride,
A protégé convened their spellbound side –
Hera, the patroness of Argos, and
Athena, was named Boiotian Guardian!

Still, their distance were kept, mute their affair,
And pleasure comes from looking from the air,
But Aphrodite, loving all smiling
Lips and eyes, cleaves toward her man, warding.

Warding off peril from him, Trojan fine,
Though death charmed him already as a sign,
Yet she saves him, from that sharp-edged spear,
From the mist covered the prince out the leer.

Clearly, Menelaos, whom Ares backs,
Has won the battle and the prize of lux!
So far this venture made everyone fend,
Thus, consider how this matter should end.

Should misery come again, once again,
And bring another war, flawfast refrain,
Or make a white banner, a pact sustain,
Such an amity both countries attain?

If such will please thee, all of you to this,
Life must also go on in Priam's knees,
While Menelaos to Helen sail home,
With the gold of Trojan treasury flam."

But in that remark, the fair goddesses rung,
Rebellious against the mighty god's twang,

For, peace they don't want for the men of Troy,
But tear them mischief and wholly destroy.

And though she held her tongue, quitting clamor,
A deep anger sullen beneath her more,
This filled Athena against her father,
But Hera, in vexation, thus utter:

"Your majesty, sorrow adrift with me,
All my toil in this matter comes to see
But the nothingness, forlorn against me
The sweat I sweated, a soft cloud to thee?

All my breathless horses, panting cold,
Just for this matter come true to behold,
When I called out that army bearing arm,
Against Priam and his sons, should they harm!

Act then if you must, but I may not serve,
Your proposal to this, I don't deserve."
Annoyed yet the king to Hera's coldness,
He took some words and enravish the rest:

"Thou art strange! It would be a ruin, say,
And yet how would Priam and his sons may
Hurt you? You wanted to trim with passion
This stronghold of power, town Illion!

Could you breach the gates and its great walls then,
To feed Priam and all his sons, and lend
All the Trojan dished their plates raw and meat,
To appease their slur, and season their feet?

So, do as you wish to do, be it so,
This dispute should I not hear again though,
However, one thing I must tell, and opt
To remember it. Listen thus a lot.

This matter, whatever it turns about,
A lust for demolishing some place out,
A hand against people, or king, might be,
Looking against them in vile memory,

Hamper not thy fury! Free my hands the same
As I free yours! – dust under thy name!
My will prevailing, although in my heart,
An unwilling nerve cannot make it start.

Wide-eyed Athena, answered in disdain:
"Three cities are beloved to me in chain,
Mykene, at the broad plain Argolis,
Of Argos and Sparta, my golden kiss.

Pull their walls down, and the golden chair too,
If you find them hateful, do as you do,
Yet, worry nay, I would not interfere,
These cities yet mine, in thy powers fear!

And still, I would not grudge on you for these,
Still am I, my consent has not at least
The power you hold, that I may cease from,
And yet, would gain nothing, lacking or awesome.

My labor, though, should remain as it is,
Should these acts I've done, unthwarted at least,
I am immortal the same as you do,

Your stock and mine are the same as you knew!

Our father Kronos, found of crooked wit,
Engendered me for purpose I befit,
To hold exalted rank since the day of birth,
And by my standing as your queen!   The girth

Of this truth cannot be expulsed or killed,
Though we are gods, these things are done and
willed,
And you're the lord of all of all immortal gods,
But come, we'll give way each other the odds

In this affair – Thus, I shall yield on you,
And you shall yield on me, fairly as hue,
The gods will follow, fate's a mocking loud,
Only be quick! Send Athena abound

Down the armies to make the Trojans tail,
That is, Trojans, not Akhaians: To fail
Not asunder the truce they swore before,
And follow the pact they are given for."

To Athena, confounded these words flew,
Briskly, the father of man and gods do:
"In all haste, down you go, amidst the cause,
To see if Trojan will sunder the truce."

To Athena is given her will to do,
Grey-eyed Athena left the council due,
As though a son of Kronos flashing light,
A sign in the heaven, an awesome sight.

Men from the deep sea, or broad army jest,
This streak of radiance, sparkling in the west,
Down she flashed, a light lining in the sky,
Amidst the troops asks, her presence to 'why'?

Wonder gazed held them, the Trojan breakers
And the Akhaians fit in armored wears,
You might hear one man says to another:
"O glorious heaven, how are we to care?

What fate is it to come: bad days ahead,
In the battle line, cast this bloody mead,
Or, can both sides be friends, forgetting vile,
Which of this, Zeus, would render for a while?

He holds the key to the knowledge of it,
What tomorrow keeps, his trident may lit."
That was the question, the armies confused,
Trojans and Akhaians fighting for news.

Athena disguised as a soldier man,
That of Laodokos, Antenor's son,
A burly spearman, brawny Trojan he,
Athena looks around, in a hurry.

She looks for Pandaros, noble a son,
She passed the mighty line of the Trojans.
Until, find him she did, waiting with troops,
Covered with shields, fresh from Aisepos,

Near him, she took her stand, and sharp words fly:
"Pandaros, son of Lykaon, I pry
You good cheers and mighty words, flowing wise,

A fame for your name, shall in gold, belies.

In my mind, something good may tempt upon,
Yet only a brave heart of a real man!
Have you a gall to send an arrow fast
Like a fork of lightning, ruining lashed?

Home against Menelaos on that part,
See, that every Trojan would rise their heart,
And every man would praise your act of might,
Especially Alexandros! By light,

Glittering gifts will surely come enthrone,
If he would see Menelaos brought down
By the keen of your bow, in bloody dire,
Bedded dolorous a sweltering pyre.

Come, fearless archer, brace yourself valiant,
Pay Apollo, the bright archer, a stunt,
Then homeward thou Zeleia with a lamb,
This, thy offer the perfect hekatomb!"

That, bemusing under her astuteness,
Athena made the archer's wit, no less,
Unto witless glory, and vanity,
The archer, hearing this, response quickly!

A polished horn from an ibex he got
One day in a game, under cover shot
At the ribs and killed it fast, on the spot,
This, man Pandaros, has keen eyes a lot.

About four feet long, the arrow horn done,

Tightly fitted, polished and bow, it span,
Capped in tips with gold, deadly as it pierce
Through the body cold, the pain of death's fierce.

This weapon now, against the ground, is tight,
Pandaros bent and strung, pointing his might,
While his men, at the same time, shielded up,
Hides him among the Argives, near his lap.

He bared his quiver, feathered arrow top,
Keen as a wave of pain this deadly craft,
Smoothly on the string bow, fitting it well,
Then pray to Apollo, Olympos dwell.

Promising intensely, his first-born lamb,
Upon his return home, this hekatomb.
He pinched the grooved butt and the string, is fixed,
And pulled evenly till the string affixed

Near his nipple. The arrowhead shall fly,
The iron touched the bow reading the sky,
Aft the tension made half a circle pass,
There, that arrow made the whipping its last.

It sang the air, like finger on it string,
But in a straight note, a flash and whizzing,
Needlesharp to the air, the arrow pinned,
Flashing through the crowd, winding through its hint.

But Menelaos, beloved he seems,
The gods neglected him not nor his skin,
For as Athena giving bliss, moved a pinch
Swerving the arrow line some lucky inch!

O that Hope of Soldiers, Athena was,
Moved Menelaos an inch away fast,
That is how a mother settled her child,
When he sleeps happily, in tame or wild –

Thus, Athena guided the arrow head
Down the golden belt buckled on his length,
The bitter arrow nicked the well-sewn pelt,
And cuts itself into the cuirass belt.

Whereas, it stuck there, passing its way through
His loin-guard, next to his belly; it flew
Off the shielded metal, that save him most,
Yet a skin is gouged, not his soul is lost.

Then rippling blood dark in a clouded stain,
Down from the wound, in the old bear remain,
As when a Meionian or a Karian
Woman dyes clear ivory to the sun,

To be a chariot's cheekpiece, ready war,
Through horseman after horseman kept a par,
Lies at the storetoom, doubling its amount,
For a great lord to achieve paramount!

Such an adornment to the driver's pride,
Glory to the ivory thigh! Abide
Menelaos to the mortal swelling,
Dyed and suffused with his dark blood running.

Unto his shins and ankles the blood flows,
Thus, Agamemnon shuddered awe, bellows

His breath to see the dark blood flowing wound,
As Menelaos himself went to cold.

But when he saw the lashing iron made,
Barbs outside its swell as the wound is flange,
Then life comes back to his face and his soul,
And warmth greeted him again from its gall.

Meanwhile the troops heard, groans of his brother,
Holding his hand, and heard him say: "I dare
To say, the truce we made is death for you,
Dear brother, should be matter dark and true.

I sent you alone, and to fight for us,
And to our nation bring glory, you must!
But lo! How they stumble our pact to dust,
And went under their heels, these Trojans rashed.

But not for nothing when we sworn our oath,
And split the lamb's blood and red wine, we sought
Each other's hands joined them to trust this rite,
And called upon a prayer do it right.

No, no, if not an Olympian bring now
The exacted punishment these bestow,
Then, he will in his good time, pay the due,
That etched this misdeed and shame after you!

They, and their wives, and children shall pay back!
For this, I know in my heart and soul: mock
Not the day when holy Illion cry,
For old meisery's abundant supply!

When fire and sword unto Priam's perish,
Good lance against its people, it vanquish!
For, Zeus, the son of Kronos, benched instill,
Against those who breached contracts as they will.

So it must be.   But this time, in anguish,
I would incur this bad faith to vanish,
Yet, if you measure the mortal time left,
And you die, I assure you, shall I wept.

Backward in shame, in depths unknown, I went
To go in the droughts of Argos to spend
The rest of time, wandering off in wail,
When in this journey, I ended up to fail.

Should we, Akhaians leave this land behind,
And so as Helen, for the Trojans find?
To stay here with Priam's glory, and gold,
While you decay here, rotting where you fold?

And your mission unachieved, shall you pass,
In our history, your name's but a dust?
I see some arrogant Trojan laughing
On the grave where you are dumped unheeding!

These men saying: 'Let Agamemnon's rage
In every sense come out like this! He stage
To bring the Akhaian army for zilch,
And sailed back hoeward Argos in their ships.

And had leave great Menelaos behind'…
Well, someone will say it, if this confide,
But let the vast earth yawn in such dismays,

When I can't leave behind this poltroon place!"

But red-haired Menelaos, said to thee:
"Calm, my brother. Courage do not hurry
To alarm the troops this insanity!
The point has hit no vital spot on me.

The golden belt stopped the arrow endorsed
On my loins, and the loin-guard stiff and coarse
With plates, hammered strong and utility,
The smith made its work, say, diligently."

Says Agamemnon: "You are right, brother,
But the wound – we'll have a surgeon take care,
Clean and dress it, with medicine for pain."
He called Talthybios, and said this plain:

"Quickly as you can, bring Makhaon here,
Let that man examine my brother dear,
O son of Asclepios, the great healer,
A master bowman made this cheerless err!

This is a defeat for their enemy,
Sorely a pain that we should all worry."
So Talthybios went, looking for him,
Amidst the army, rank heavy and slim.

Then, as he found the healer, standing tall,
With troops around him, like shield and a wall,
Among men from Trike the grazing land,
Approaching him, the crier made his stand:

"Son of Asclepios, Agamemnon says,

Examine Menelaos, wounded lays,
A master bowman has wounded of him.
You are summoned quickly, time should not win!

'This is a defeat for their enemy,
Sorely a pain that we should all worry.'"
Thus stirred at the message Makhaon run,
Toward the red-haired captain groaning shun.

Gathered around him, stood Akhaian peers,
And pulled the arrow free, against his sneers,
The barb broke off as it comes out the wound,
Half the pain Makhaon' soft hands withstood.

He unbuckled the golden belt, hammered
Plates of loin-guard, and saw the arrow's bled,
He suck the wound, then he sprinkled some balm,
That Kheiron gave to his father no sham.

While tending Menelaos, wardcry lord,
Trojan ranks reformed formation and sword,
Then the Akhaians put their armors too,
Mindful of the battle, the war is due.

In that hour, unstoppable is the clash,
None can stop Agamemnon's bloody bash,
Not a moment's torpor, malign them set,
A fiery ardor for battle of death!

This, man's honor gained, and honor reflect,
Now, the war comes, heaven and earth expect
Had not the gods under pride and conceit,
The pact is done, and sail the Trojan leaves.

Agamemnon left his consort to check,
With his chariot run, gleaming bronze effect,
His driver, Eurymedon, honored lad,
Son that Ptolemaios Peiraides had.

Round they reined, with snorting horses this time,
Agamemnon inspect the marshalled prime,
Bring the chariot up when weariness came,
Should his legs, after the inspection, flame.

On foot, he ranged around, forming his band,
The charioteer units he saw stood and dand,
Says Agamemnon to the charioteers:
"Argives, keep your courage up – straight and fierce!

Zeus has no luck for liars, backs them nay!
But now, stir up the Akhaians today
Stir up in battle, as quickly as we can,
The Trojans thawed the truce, betray a hand!

Again, death to the Trojans, curse their spears,
Bad times ahead for those who had them fears,
They overrode our pact and broken it,
Stir the army up – to Trojan's defeat!"

On seeing any slack, unready hearts,
Those who hated war, he lashed them with darts,
With these words he told, in anger, he toned:
"Rabbit hearts of Argos! Thy weak enthroned!

Are you not dead in shame, breathless as dust?
How can you stand there stunned as a deer must?

Like a deer chased all day, until it last,
And droop and halted broken as time passed?

This, how you look, running cowards to fight,
Will you stand until Priam made delight
Of your fear, and overran our ships home?
And breached above our great men, few or some,

To find out if Zeus' hands has spelt your fall?
And writ their names above ours in that wall?"
So as their commander, reviewed their will,
Passing along the crowded rank and fill.

Along the Kretans, he passed, with their heart,
Putting on their armor, its warcries start!
Around was Idomeneus, wild boar strong,
A great captain, his company along.

At the rear was Meriones, likewise did,
The Lord Marshall elated by this deed,
Said to Idomeneus in warmest tone:
"Idomeneus, thou art a man I prize,

Above all horsemen, your kind stands ahead,
Whether in war, in blood awed summer shed,
Or in labor thy fruitful sweat adored,
Or in feasts where thy company adorned.

Where wine is mixed in bowls, reserve for us,
O councilors of war, thy honor lasts!
Akhaian gentlemen unshorn of hair,
May gulped their wine portions down; but your share

Is filled up, and shall be filled up again,
But now the feast is war – in this, remain,
Just like mine! For we are moved just the same,
As you do for the wake of Trojan shame!

To this, Idomeneus, round the rest,
Answered: "Son of Atreus, more than best
Shall I stand by you – to this, I swear,
My heart and soul the same, in this affair!

But now, stir up the Akhaian armies
As quickly as you can, this Trojans peace
We cannot give them sure; the pact is torn,
And the victors today in us reborn!"

Happy to such a firm relay he heard
This fierceness of great Atreus, unshattered!
Then came he on two Ajax, tall and short,
Buckling on their gears, their bravery of worth!

Around them armed the same buckling their arms,
The cloud of infantry ready, alarmed,
Just when a dark cloud sprung in the fair sky,
The hilltop shepherd beware of its sigh,

Until the west wind in distant beware,
And a fiercer pitch back clouds greets the lair,
With lightning squalls driven along its front,
Shivering though, he drives his flock.

Into a cavern sheltering them strong!
Grim as that were these dense dark cloud along,
Armed for war, armed for lightning, mighty hold,

With these Ajaxes, honor bright as gold!

Their arms of shield pitch black and hedge of spear,
Spiny were these, its victim lamed sincere,
Lord Agamemnon, heartened at this sight,
Spoke to his captains, tenderous and pleased!

Says he: "Ajax and Ajax, captains of Argos,
Shield and armed in your honorsmith of golds,
I have no orders for you, until yet,
No need to put on your whole parapet.

Such honor and mood to your troops is passed,
O Father Zeus, goddess Athena must
Bring men as these! O Apollo the great,
Bring more fearless men in our women's fate!

Down to Priam's high wall fortress, comrades!
Taken down in one day plundered, our raids!
Down to Trojan army, the truce they've break,
And unto Menelaos' wound that ache!"

With this he left, passing on the latter,
He found Lord Nestor the Pylian master,
The great orator, haranguing the men
From steads of Pylos, finest harbor land!

Around him were the captains Pelagon,
Alastor, Khromios, Bias and Haimon.
Charioteers he sent forward, strong as wall,
And kept the infantry behind install.

Thus, weak and coward men between the brave,

That we may fight forcibly till their grave,
This, the chariotmen instructed to go,
First in the battle, like vanguard, they grow.

Such formation kept the line straight and strong,
No tangle, no cut off, in all its throng,
The chariots run like arrows smoothing field,
The dust on their wheels, magnifying shield!

Says, "But none should rely on horsemanship,
Where bravery attacks through wheels it whip!
Much less a soldier who retreat alone,
When chariot no longer carries his throne.

For with this, the soldier in death, might cry
To the utter punch of woe, as he sigh
Along valor that relies on his horse,
And bravery that dishonor the cause.

But let every brave man line with their lance,
Hold their bravery, as to war they dance,
In this, man's courage lunged against their fear,
And power's intimate, as it is dear!

In the old days, I have thought of greatness,
Not for myself, but for these warriors' best,
Where cities are shades of gloom and despair,
Falling before like ashes in the air!

Such is the course of men, enough to say,
Where courage is fittingly on its way,
If kept in mind, this plan would take its role,
When fought in courage, victory is whole."

The old man's exhortation, arose in fire,
From a long years of shrewdness and desire,
In this ways of war, utmost is his skill,
Lord Nestor the brave, wisest in the hill!

Such acclaim gladdened Agamemnon's heart,
To him, approving these words: "O brave heart,
That's what I 'm looking for: if only strong
Were your legs, as your years before, along,

When the same force abodes within thy arm,
Only that I wish that it remains warm,
And your strength is whole again, I say wise,
But time's no longer, and wrinkling belies,

Where it would be better for some to be
In that age of yours, where time has been wee,
And better then your age be younger still,
Where you're still young, fullest in all thy will!"

Nestor, the earl of Gereneia, bade,
The old charioteer, honored, wise, thus said:
"Agamemnon, 'tis better in my part,
And wish long enough, to strengthen this heart,

That I too would become his great name be,
Who killed Ereuthalion to victory,
But immortal gods, hallowed above us,
Has set men to weigh their own gold and trash.

My youth is claimed, and my manhood ordained,
Now, my age has come to ripe, shall I bane?

Nay, but here, I have my place, to its last,
Take the chariot, and the council entrust,

I commanded them, and they obeyed me,
For me, that is sure enough heavenly,
Duties these are for an elderly man,
Follow my advice, shield on, do not run!

Good lancers abound, countless in your head,
Good spears they must have, deadly as they spread,
But men who were born later should they speak,
Younger men should listen well, trust him meek!"

Then the son of Atreus heard him out,
And passed along a glad approving heart.
Next found him Menestheus, Peteos son,
Surrounded by mighty Athenians.

This man's good hand in battle rise with fame;
Near him, the great Odysseus, fully-aimed,
Along with Kephallenians, rounding rank,
Waiting for word of battle reach their flank.

Yet only the first wall, rippled affront,
In the blood scattered roads and ghastly rant,
The troops of Odysseus stood in waiting,
As though they waited long undesiring,

Lord Agamemnon, marshall of chaos,
Saw this action, he cried: "Son of Peteos,
Reared in the hammock of the gods, sire!
You, Odysseus, hero I most desire,

Master of guile and greed, this troop you bring,
Why both submissive and so retiring?
Why they wait for other troops to go first,
Have not their valor already in thirst?

The two of you, in action, should be first,
In the blaze of trumpets, and fiery verse,
In the shadows of combat, echoing,
The same does the rhythm of our feasting!

Where you be the last to stand amongst us?
Or the first to stand aloof in combats?
When the sound of our battlecry is heard,
Among the valiant, are you not prepared?

You and the officers heard me more than
The great many soldiers herein at hand,
On our feast, my words flew on you instant,
And you come before the whole Akhaians!

And this is what you like: roasted meat and cups,
Festive toast of honeyed-wine and pure saps!
What you desire, it flew instantly yours,
And the night is ended contented hours.

But now, have you not prepared the valor,
And the strength within you perished a sore?
That gladly you wait for ten troops ahead,
To move forward, attack with bronze naked?

When you should be the first in line of them,
Bound in strength fiercer a lion can't claim!
But waiting a word from me, troublous ires,

Makes my heart faint, and your glory retires!"

Odysseus, cunning commander scowled thus,
Answered him guileful, as he must: "Alas,
Son of Atreus, I must say you right,
What panicked you with these words not upright?

How can you say, my honor fights in vain,
Or let this fight ran away just that plain?
Have we not, at this time, whet our spears
Against the Trojans, in this edge, ninth year?

Well, if you want to see me, hand-in-hand,
Combat in the front line, as you demand,
Then I, father of Telemakhos, roar,
Your bluster is all wind, whispering lore!"

Then, Lord Agamemenon, thinking it twice
The words he just uttered that seems unwise,
Replied he, beaming, a bright facial smile,
Taking back his hassles, from just a while:

"Son of Laertes, warrior covered in gold,
Reared in the hammock of the gods of old!
Thou, O master mariner, soldier-prince,
I would, in all fairness, should I convince,

That, I need not give you orders and notes,
Or hand you the plans, handle you with guts,
For well-verse, and well-disposed, as you are,
Of my thoughts, I need not tell what they are.

Indeed, your thought in semblance, has at least,

So I say, 'Come, shall I amend of this,'
If I told you words uncalled for your thought,
I shall ask the seawind to blow them off!"

Thus, the king left, gone amidst the soldiers,
Where Diomedes, son of gallant heirs,
Of Tydeus, in wheels ready for combat,
And all pedigree of horses around,

With plenty of discipline, standing still,
With Sthenelos nearby, waiting for his kill,
In the glimpse of them, spoke the war master,
Rebuke this son of Kapaneus, and snare:

"Arcane! Baffled deeply in this obscure,
O Tydeus, breaker of horses! I'm sure
You stand there still, but lo, have you been shy?
So cautious, wary what forth fate belie?

Your father, Kapaneus, shunt not like this,
Stand still, wait for others to move their knees,
But he rather fight alone, braving all,
Ahead of other soldiers, and their soul!

For as they said, he rather toil in war,
Than win a war without touching a par,
Well, I have not met him, nor laid my eyes,
But they said, he had no peer or disguise!

In peace, as Polykenikes' ally told,
Hunting troops, he entered Mykene old,
At that time, marching on, besieging walls
Of ancient Thebes, down their glory and halls,

Came him appealing for first-rate soldiers,
To bring down Thebes, our people gladly fairs,
And would have granted his plea, but Zeus
Through an omen, speaks; thus changes the ruse,

And made the people changed their mind rethink,
It blinked their eyes, what color's in the ink.
So, taking the road, a stout army spread,
At Asopos, where he laid his grassy bed.

Beside his lay flows a deep river rush,
And they ordered Tydeus, cunningly hush,
Forwarding their message, he found certain
The Kadmeians thronging their entertain,

A feast in Eteokles handsome sandstone,
Where, amidst his company, went alone,
And without liege, comrade, or distant friend,
He went along the way, yet unafraid!

He challenged them to wrestle, beating all,
Easy as a fire consume a wood stall,
Only thus, being seconded by her,
Great Athena, the Kameians despair.

Yet they made traps for him, on his way back,
Fifty men deployed in a sturdy mock,
Under two leaders, the ploy they insist,
Maion, immortal-seeming son, assists

Polyphontes, son of Autophonos,
These goaders of horses, angered and tossed,

Bring about Tydeus' fate a wanting end,
But listen, the twist, of things that happened!

For, Tydeus brought them all to grief and death,
Except for one man, Maion, whom he spared,
And he sent home, as gods bid him obey,
And this is your father, Tydeus, I say.

Yet this Aitolian, great must be his name,
Weaker than he in war a man ashame,
Whom he fathered; yet, he stands there proudly,
Waiting for others in the assembly!"

Diomedes, the rugged man, assents,
Said nothing whatsoever. But laments
Sthenelos, retorting the words he spoke,
Says: "Atreides, why distort things a rogue?

A man who knew well how to be so just,
But we say, we're far better than the last,
Far better than our fathers would have done,
Not they, but we, took Thebes with our hands,

And down their seven gates, harrowing all,
Yet with smaller force against heavier wall,
We made them submit to our very name,
And that made us honored in timeless fame.

Is this not Zeus' portents? The signs from gods.
But our fathers? What have they done are odds,
Their own recklessness destroyed their old name,
Aye, they destroyed their own fathers to shame!

Now, how would you rate them equal to us?
Not at any chance." Now Diomedes,
With a frown turned aside, saying proud,
In a voice thunderous, mightily loud:

"O comrades, men of the Old Horse, be still,
Believe me, the blame should not be our kill,
I take not this ill, our Lord Marshall's ill,
But as he must goad us to fight his will:

For the glory goes to him endlessly,
When Trojan walls and manors fell drowsy,
And we triumph this powerful city,
Thus, the anguish goes to him, as we flee

And scattered our losses, our men be slain,
When that powerful city triumph, pain
To his heart, or joy to his soul? Come,
Both of us should wear valor, nay a sham."

Then off he bound on his chariot uphold,
In full armor, in his chest bronze and gold,
A captain roused against the ground for war,
Even a stout heart would have fear a scar.

Down upon the shore of echoing surf,
Amidst the cooling clouds, covering turf,
The bellows of the west wind, made big waves,
Looming unto the open sea; it raves

The shore with bubbles and foaming circles,
Around the surging lines and briny shells,
In the spumes of seawater, refreshing,

The wild tremble against their silent string.

So, the Danaäns formed their positions,
And rose relentless toward their actions,
Ah, toward the Trojans, against their wall,
Every captains, forwarding, as they call.

The troops were mainly silent, as the tide,
Strong though silent, unassuming their side,
Unto their captains, docile and passive,
Thus, what you would see, you may not believe!

A great army, with their warcries below,
Noiseless against their march, silently raw,
Most of them docile to their captains great,
Agamemnon, had his words in bad shape!

On the other side, the Trojans were not,
A strong voice runs like a spear minted hot,
Against their enemies, shattering hearts,
This strong voice went up loud before it starts!

Like the flocks clustered innumerable
On a rich man's list, waiting for a poll,
To yield their milk white, and bleating loudly,
Rousing others' bleats, and continually.

Just so the Trojans rose through all the foe,
Not as a single voice in height or low,
Not as a single tongue, but mingled blast
Of voices of men from many lands.

This great army, god Ares urged upon,

On other side, grey-eyed Athena run,
With Terror and Rout, brewing them to fight,
And Hate, moving their hearts in dimming light.

This insatiable sister-in-arms stand
Against his brother's man-destroying hand,
Frail at first, unable to call aloud,
But growing, she rear her head through the gods

In heaven and walked the earth. Until then,
She sowed ferocity, and cruel men,
Crossing the ranks of soul, redoubling cries,
Their groans for hatred, is not surprise!

The long lines of men met like two great walls
Colliding against each other, it rolls
Like stones crumbling each other's strength and form,
Shocks of bull's hide, battering pikes, and storm

Of men's bronze, of chariot's reins, and their spears,
These met together in a line forbears,
A great din arose, as men destroying
And destroyed buckled their breath and dying.

The earth streamed with blood, warm against the
plain,
In one thrilled of agony and pain!
In spring, snow-water torrents flowing wild,
Rushing mighty rivers and gorges filled,

And far away the shepherd, on a hill
Is able to hear the roar, as he sealed
His eyes, and listen to what it intends,

The same is the sound, such clamor assents.

Antilokhos down the first Trojan halt,
A brave man in the front line, enthralled,
Ekhepolos Thalysiades unveiled
The darkness when Antilokhos' sword nailed

On his forehead, that down him to his death,
On his ridge, driven, bore his noble crest,
As his point went through helmet, and bone,
Such that darkness met him instantly done.

He toppled like a tower, helplessly,
In awe, the chief of Abantes decree
To haul and grab him out of the warfield,
And strip him quickly, swiftly in his yield,

Thus the trial is brief, a blink, a splash,
For while he tugged the corpse, in bloody wash,
His flank exposed beside, easy as prey,
There, Agenor took the moment to slay!

The spear he shod, and death bites the dragger,
Hit him on the flank, ends a crumpled chair,
As he lose his breath, a bitter rage roamed
On top of his body, a bloody tomb!

Between Akhaians and Trojans raging,
His heart ceases, and the last words dying,
For like wolves above him, as whirling howls,
Against each other, sudden joy and growls!

Then, Ajax Telemonios knocked down strong,

Son of Anthemion, Simoeisios – long
His time, should have been for him, only that,
In the full of bloom of his youth, age is not.

Ajax killed the youth, and flowers unbloom'd
On his name, his seeds are all abandoned: -
On the slopes of Ida, descending knolls,
By the bank Simoeis, his fate recalls.

Along this place, her mother conceived him,
While tending the flocks, he got his name firm,
Yet, with Ajax's shaft, his life is cut short,
And nobody know squares what would be his worth.

For, brave this young man, in the lead he came,
And accept the spear thrust squarely aim,
Beside the nipple, right side, pierces him,
And the bronze point, made his spirit a trim.

Reeled and fell in the dust, that very day,
In the great meadow, asking for his lay.
Like a poplar growing on bottom lands,
When a wild fire begun to taste the blands,

Not a bending clue for his winding tear,
Nor a nectar-filled bee to hint some fear,
The chariot-builder's ax, shining iron,
Made it like lion, his life's the carrion.

And so, down it moves to the river,
So he vanquished the youth instantly shared
The glory of hatred when used to kill
Has no respect on one's future or will.

Then, Aias in his turn, a son of king,
Priam's son Antiphos, thus glittering,
His cuirass against the light made some blaze,
He tried to spear Aias, but missed his trace,

Instead he hit Leukos, in his groin,
This comrade of Odysseus' mighty loin,
Wrought in fury upon his futile death,
Dropped out of his grasp, and fell on the earth.

Flashing though his helmet, Odysseus stand,
Shouldering fury, ruining a good hand,
Yet, play at his lance, glowers right and left,
And made the Trojans recoil with their breath.

And one of the son of Priam, he cast
No wasted motion and hit that bastard bust,
A certain Demokoön, from Abydos,
Where he kept his horses, a seldom lose,

Odysseus' heart is full of rage over
The death of his companion, with his spear
Passed into the temple, spearheaded,
So darkness veiled his eyes, certainly dead.

As Demokoön fell, he thumped at the ground,
And his armor clanged upon him, the sound
Of weary, to a sensitive cadence,
His spears bade farewell with his unused lance!

The Trojans march on, gave way to advance,
Prince Hektor too, braving the deadly dance,

While they advanced, the Argives made their yell,
Dragging dead men off to unleash the hell.

Now from Pergamos, god Apollo cried,
In indignation, to the Trojans' pride:
"Forward! Trojans, O breakers of horses,
Show your enemies how a warlord press!

Will you bow in fury against these foe?
See, they are not made of iron or stone
To make your spears shy, your lances worried!
See too, Akhilles is not fighting with,

But tasting wrath by himself, in the shore,
Beside his ship, filling his heart more,
O Trojans, breakers of horses, march on,
Forward! Don't let the Akhaian move on!"

That terrible god Ares, shouts above,
In his tower bellowing strength! Then move
Tritogeneia, splendid daughter of Zeus,
Lifting the hearts of Akahaians bemused.

For, while many hearts she saw well-dismayed,
She lifted them up, in war mode she placed,
Both armies heightened by fury and hate,
Armed in bloody hands, veiled and sunken fate.

Thus, fate calls upon mighty Diores
Amarungkeides, veiled his eyes to rest,
A jagged stone hits him, his ankle disturbed,
Peiros Imbrasides, his life's dissolved.

This Thracian captain from Airos has bled,
With the stones, crushing both tendons instead,
That the tall man tumbled down in the dust,
Flinging wide his arms, to his comrades passed,

Yet panting his life away, Peiros run
To gash the spear in his bellybutton,
His bowels spilled in the horrid of sight,
And darkness veiled his eyes out of the light.

Then, Thoas the Aiotolian onward
Rushed against Peiros lunging his spear hard,
Hitting him above the nipple, he struck,
And the pointed bronze in his lung unlocked.

Thoas at a close, wrench his heavy spear,
Pulled it out of the chest, the bloody cheer,
Then as he drew his sword, and killed him with
A stroke on the belly, he could not meet,

His gear could not rip the dead man's body,
His friends repulsed Thoas' arms in fury,
Closing round until he gave down and die,
At the end of the line, our warriors lie.

As for the two, laying rest on the dust,
Captains of the Thracians and Epeians!
Both hinted in bronze, and killed by the spear,
While down too many around them appear.

Thereafter, not a man is scorned or bled,
In that fight no expert of battle is ahead,
Who might go well untouched by any way,

Unscathed in any bronze or spear that day.

A witness, thus, led by Athena's might
Shielded by her from stones and arrow's flight,
That day, Trojans and Akhaians thronged vast,
Beside each other's blood, prone in the dust.*

SOMETHING ABOUT ILION
BOOK V
CONGREGATION OF THE MIGHTY

Diomedes' hour struck the moment great,
Athena embolden his name and fate,
To tower confidence amidst the war,
And win glory, is not a distant far.

On his shield and helm is Athena's fire,
Kindled like the midsummer's scorching ire,
The flaming star of heaven matching this,
Rising in the sky, bathed in Ocean's mist.

So fiery she made his head glow aloud,
And his shoulders stronger than he might sound,
She impelled him go to the heavy mass,
Where the greatest number fought, as it was.

A rich man, Dares, noble Trojan man,
Favorfast to Hephaistos had two sons,
Well-trained in war, Phegeus and Idaios,
Sent to the warfare, heirs yet, they must choose.

These two, the Akhaian faced gladly well,

They came forward down the chariot they quell,
Diomedes, on foot come braced on them,
Distance narrowing, the brothers on them.

Phegeus moved first, he aimed his spear a shout,
Then casted assuredly the long spear out,
But it failed to pin on the man he spot,
Where his left shoulder repels its old plot.

Diomedes cleared, his turn came at once,
He wheeled his spear high, fly the bronze-shod lance
Toward Phegeus' stand! Nay, it missed him nipped,
Between his nipples knocking him adrift,

Backward to his men, a frightful unease,
Idaios as a revenge against, gist
His beautiful chariot, leaping down craze,
His brother's life is taken off and razed.

But nay, he fright to stand where his lad lays,
Or surely, death shall elude him a haste,
Unless Hephaistos performed a rescue,
And hide him in the darkness, without a clue.

To spare his father's grief, his lost severe,
Pulling the horses' head, lashing with fear,
So instead, Diomedes handed it
To his team, where it should go to the ship!

When the Trojans saw how Dare's sons fared,
One saved from Diomedes' hands, the snared,
The other lying dead beside his car,
Every man misgave their hope for this war.

Grey-eyed Athena took Ares' hands, say:
"Ares, misery of all mankind, lay
Your virtue upon that sight, I contend,
O crusted in blood, I was so offend!

Why not let both armies to fight alone,
Allow them ensure victory for their own?
Why not? – Zeus' glory may hold out the champ,
And we clear the combat, we clear the cramp.

And his rage may not touch this war's affair,
Who amongst the armies should dare he spare "
She led him at the battle though she spoke,
At Skamander's side they sat at this yoke.

Bold the Akhaian forced the Trojans back,
Every captain faithfully kill and knock,
The blood thirst has not stop, ever from them,
Both armies roam their fury at the hem.

First, Lord Agamemnon to Odios struck,
A tall Halizones warior he crack,
From his chariot wheels crash this warrior's rack,
Signaling retreat when a spear was struck,

That, as he had turned, Agamemnon's spear
Went through his chest, a straight line from the rear,
Between his shoulders, the iron is cursed,
Down he crash with the clanging and his thirst!

Idomeneus killed the warrior Phaistos,
From a farmland Tarne, son of Boros,

So, as the man rose upon his chariot,
Idomeneus drove through rashing riot,

Dipping through the right rein, Phaistos tumbled,
Out of his car, numbling darkness fabled,
Shrouding him the dim clouds, as Kretans
Took his gear, loot the other dead Trojans.

Then, the great hunter Skamandrios
Known as the hunter son of Strophios,
Has fell on Menelaos' point and edge,
Down the ground he fondled his fury's stretch.

This hunter expert, Skamandrios
Whom Artemis herself taught skillful bows,
To bring down antelopes, deer, many games,
Bred in the forests and hills, wilds and tames.

Though he knew his skills and ravishing art,
Not even Artemis would help him out,
She who fills the air with blameless arrows,
Or his own good shooting will save his cause.

For, furious Menelaos thrust him dead
Between his shoulders, and pushed his cold head,
His ribs are worn-out and crashed, down he fell,
His armor clanging, notwithstanding hell.

Then, Meriones killed handy Phereklos,
Son of Hermonides, artist utmost,
He who knew all manner of building art
And Handicraft, Phallas Athena's heart.

O great he built the fatal ships enclosed
His Trojan warships for Alexandros,
Yet now, heaven's will is silent as dust,
Its waters are foaming, his time has passed:

As Meriones hit him on the buttocks,
Pierced his bladder with his cold spear-steel shocks,
He missed the pelvic bone, yet still the end
Of Phereklos' artistic compliment.

He fell moaning, numbing his hands and knees,
And death shrouded him, tears of recessed his,
How suffering from war causes uncheers,
One's pride, unto another man, is fierce.

Then Meges unto Pedaios attend,
The bastard son of Lord Antenor, and
A son whom Lady Theano prized well,
Equal to his own, be pleased in his dwell.

Meges Phyleides, master spearman rock,
Runs close to him, and through his nape he struck,
The point cleave his tongue and against his teeth,
Biting the cold bronze, he fell in the pit.

In the ground laid his corpse, awestruck, surprised,
An enemy-wise hit him from behind.
So his eye was veiled in darkness and dim,
Unable to speak his curses and dream.

Then Eurypylos Euaimonides
Brought Hypsenor down, his blood in his vest,
Hypsenor, son of Dolophion, a priest

Of Skamander in the old time's mist,

Honored by the folk as if he's a god,
Time immemorial, such wisdom is sod,
In the bright arms of the sun, priests define,
The words of god, and man's fate they confine.

As his foe fled, Eurypylos leapt high
And draw his sword as he run, bloody dry,
Cutting him in the bronze and shoulder blade,
In blood, the arm dropped, surging breaths that fade.

His destiny, unveiled by that sword quick,
Took his life, and pass unto grieving sick.
So these Akhaians toiled though rough it charged,
Winning honors from the eyes at the large.

You could not tell, as for Diomedes,
If he were Akhaian or Trojan serve,
Just as his course along the plain against,
Like April torrent fed by snow. And worst

A river under flood that sweeps away
His noble bank, erasing crags to play,
This man, as he moves along the great war,
Sweeps like instantaneous killing monster.

As a river flowing, none could hold him,
Not from the scorching sun to orchard dim,
A river suddenly rises to Zeus,
Crest higher like a flash, moving bad news.

That, many field were done, ravaged and drowned,

Beautiful grains are wasted as he frowned,
Even so Diomedes, reaping blood,
That none could hold him, just like a great flood!

Now, unto Pandaros' wit, it might end,
As he looked over him, far-reaching went,
Thus bent his bow unto Diomedes,
And shot him boldly, from among the rest.

Hitting his cuirass, his left shoulder joint,
The arrow landed safely at that point,
Spattering blood on the bronze, awestruck felt,
Then Pandaros shouts to the Trojan belt!

"Trojans forward! Come, charioteers! And see
Their Akhaian champion it hit by me!
I swear this arrowhead shall bring him down,
If that is what Apollo's cheer! Get down

You Diomedes, with this arrowhead,
Down to Akhaia must you sail and fled,
And I on my way to Lykia, shall spend
The rest of my day in the golden."

Among Trojans, he triumphantly shout,
But his arrow fumbled its way without,
Down to his foe, the arrowhead has failed,
Lucky Akhaian, the Trojan has wailed.

And so Diomedes, retires a ground,
And jests at Sthenelos, to mend his wound.
Says Diomedes: "Sthenelos, old friend,
Quick thou jump down and pull this bloody fiend,

This jabbing arrow has stuck my shoulder!"
Sthenelos domed down, and press his hands where
The jabbing arrow stuck, and drew the slim
Shaft of his wound, with staining blood – that whim

His knitted shirt these spurts of gore, all red,
Diomedes, in warcry loud, prayed:
"Oh hear me, daughter of Zeus, storm-cloud bear,
Relentless to us, tireless in power!

O tireless one, Athena, My father
Stood before you, and helped him mightier,
In all hot fight, and in this war, I pray,
Befriend me too, avenge glory today!

Bring me near that man who struck my shoulder
With his arrowhead, yet in surprise; where
He stands, bring me in range, that I may see
Who this man who sworn my death to be!"

His prayer heard, unto Athena's bound,
With lissome legs, she went to the war ground,
Standing near him, saying swiftly, she wage:
"Diomedes, forsake not thy courage!

Continue the fight against the Trojans,
This same fury I have given as lance
To your father's heart, and he never quailed,
But the foes around him, surely bewailed –

So, Tydeus, master of horses, he.
Now, as you prayed unto me, intensely,

I have already cleared the way to him
Who sworn your death with his arrow. The dim

Of the dust, and the mist blurring your eyes,
I have cleared for you, bring back his surprise,
Then, shall it be wise to distinguish god,
Or man that you may not roam in combat,

Beware, if any god may test your strength,
And the hint of courage in time, in length,
Be sure, you are not the soldier to dare,
None, except Aphrodite, beauty fair,

For, if she joined this war, wound her gravely
With your bronze spear." That moment, instantly,
Grey-eyed Athena left him, made his way,
Toward Pandaros, he too sworn to pay!

At first, the burn of fight lashes on him,
In the war against Troy, burning's it seem,
Yet now three times furious this man alive,
Burning three times, fiery three times his drive!

More than burning, but a blood-lusting leech,
But more than a leech, a lion indeed:
A wounded lion, some shepherd has done,
Made it weak for a while and wild to none.

But that, as is said, is just for a while,
That when it regains its wild claws and bile,
It leaps among its offenders and drag,
With tumult a roar, and ravishing tug.

Those who offended it run away fast
Into a cavern, where death might have passed,
And to save their lives, the flocks scattered thrown
Into the lion's claws and oblivion.

Then, abandoned, the flock bleats continuous,
In heaps, however, myriad lie confused,
Torn carcasses and carrion so fresh,
The lion satisfied itself with flesh.

And so, that wildness brought Diomedes,
To roar lion-wise, and defend his best,
Plunged unto the Trojans, wildness brought,
Nobody can stop his wild arm or foot.

Along the way he met unfrightened men,
Of foxes and lions too though these men,
But in anger burst, clashes one by one,
A fallen brood of Trojans in his hand!

First, he killed Astynoös, and a captain,
Of Hypeiron's name, one with a bronze pain
From his spear, the other struck by his sword,
Fatally wounded his collarbone mourned.

Severing his whole shoulder, blood he lost,
And their breath gathered by this monster host,
These men he met, and then brothers Abas
And Polyeidos, sons of Eurydamas.

He, being an interpreter of dreams,
Cannot, on certainty, tell what it seems,
For his sons' fate this ludicrous battle,

Silent yet for him the great oracle.

For, Diomedes killed his sons stripped down,
The blood of the brothers thicking the lawn.
Next brothers he met, Thoon and Xanthos,
Dearest warriors and sons to Phainops,

He, being a father in olden years,
Worn out of misery and doubts and fears,
For, if these his heirs would die in the war,
There's none to continue his name no more.

And yet unwittingly, Diomedes
Put this old man's doubt in its final rest,
For he killed his sons overpowering,
And that made his tears like river flowing.

Now that he is empty for heir to hold,
All days after, in mourning thus behold
This father's home now a cheerless welcome,
All his heritage scattered and alone.

Next were the sons of Dardan Priam king,
Diomedes destroyed while a-wheeling,
Their strong chariots cannot even hold him,
His wildness a thug, a brute, ruffian brim.

This, his sons, Ekhammon and Khromios,
Crunching their neck, the rashing lion caused,
While in their car, leaped his deadly armor,
And dragged the brothers down utmost fervor.

He sends the horses to the rear, and fled,

Great Diomedes, as lion he fed,
The Trojans lost of heirs, they greatly mourned,
And yet it was a war, and death is sworn.

Aineias, on a higher ground, observe,
These bloody havoc that one man has served,
He moved up the line of frightened Trojan,
And strengthen their defense as he ran

In search of Pandaros, Lykaon's mighty
Son he is, and a noble one, says he:
"Pandaros, where is your bow and your fame?
Not one from Lykia contends with your name!

Where are your fledged arrows and archery?
Not one would claim against you victory!
Here, on this day, to great Zeus, lift thy hand,
Let that arrow fly steady, shall it stand

Against that mighty fighter, as he was,
Overwhelming the finest in our class,
For whoever he is, badly he hurt
The Trojan ranks and files in anger worst!

Pandaros, again, let that arrow fly
Toward that mighty fighter, let him die!
Unless he is a god bearing a rod
That grudges and smitten our noble blood,

Against us, shall be bid a sacrifice,
And yes, his anger is wistfully thrice,
Fly that arrow, now! Avenge all our men,
Let Akhaians see how mighty we stand!"

Lykaon's noble son to him replied:
"Aineias, master of battle, I tried
To see who this mighty fighter could be,
And I think Diomedes must he be!

Thus, his helm and shield bearing his glory,
And a high plume-socket his travesty,
This I recognize before his warside,
Reflected unto me his might abide.

Should I not swear a god he must be, nay,
But some god backs him up to charge his play,
On a crazy rave he has just amend,
A god truly is behind him, a fiend.

And some god clouding his weak in stronghold,
Wrapped in stormcloud bending my bronze! Behold:
That god bent the arrow I hit on him,
That in his shoulder I have struck in clean.

I thought Death has already taken him,
For that shot is sure to wipe all his dream,
But no, some angry god save him from death,
That he has not yet face the hungry earth!

I lack from chariots and a ride, right now,
But on my father's hall, therewith the show,
Eleven chariots newly-built for use,
With housings on them all, yet I refused.

Thus, every chariot stands a team nearby
Under my command, yet I have denied,

How many great things, Lykaon told me,
Before I left his mansion in hurry,

Aye, I left them untouched, and trod on foot,
To Illion, relying on my shoot,
But all of these, I refused, for this bow –
A bow that failed not once but twice, by now!

A bow that destined me to fail and flop,
For, in this battle, two great men I shot,
They're Menelaos and Diomedes,
I drew blood on them, but only to rest

Not in the pillows of silence and calm,
But only for a while, these beasts would drum
The warcry against the whole Trojan clan,
For I rouse them more, than silence these men,

And terrible day is destined for me,
Though I count early for our victory,
And led my men for the sweet town of Troy
For Hektor's sake, but I start to destroy.

If my return is cast, and stand beyond,
To see my beautiful wife and my land,
Then, in my great hall, let someone proceed
To cut my head off, and my name is bleed.

Unless I throw the bow, break it between,
And unto a blazing fire, throw it in,
It goes with me and my name undergloom,
Useless pendant on a necklace of doom!"

Says Aeneias: "Words be not our spearman,
Talk not anymore! Till we act forbear,
We can drive the chariot against his might,
And take him on with a spear! Tell, delight

On his death, mount the chariot, and steadfast,
Look how these horses can run from the Tros!
Splendid breed, just like the blood in your vein,
Let's start to unleash fury and this rein!

This, like a veering wind, a rare pursuit,
A way like a flash, these horses can shoot,
So this would save us, the rummaging hail,
Take us Troyward if Zeus permits to tail

That man, Diomedes, into our hands,
So come, take the wheel and rein, understand?
Or you may face the man worthy to kill,
As I mind the horses, what is thy will?"

Says Lykaon: "Aeneias, hold the rein,
Manage the chariot, and the horses' vein!
The team too thou shall guide, against his troop,
For if they see us, they will make a loop,

And it would be easier to catch us
Like prey within a circle of bloodlusts,
So, let's give to Diomedes this time,
God forbid, shall they panic in your prime,

In just hearing your voice! But beware thus,
For that Diomedes' heart fearless has,
Might balk at us while we're still in the car,

And leapt over us, and leaves us a scar!

Would God forbid an act against our breath,
And relieve us of our duties, in the breadth
Of time, and the width of dreams, shall I prove,
I'll take him to lame, until he can't move!

And my good spear shall be his dying wish,
When he attacks against us, I unleash
The fury, a revenge against our best,
He may kill me, but shall I do the rest!"

Both agreed and rode the chariot toward
Diomedes, sworn to mix blood and lard!
But Sthenelos, the son of Kapaneus,
Caught sight of them, and turned to him, and loose:

"Diomedes, friend of my heart and soul,
Two spearmen approaching dare here a roll,
Big men were they, would have sworn of your blood,
Look at them, forthcoming like a storm god!

One is Pandaros the well-known bowman,
His father, but the great man Lykaon!
And the other, Aineias, mighty man,
Claims Ankhises and his fatherland,

His mother Aphrodite, goddess 'bove,
Up to you, comrade, what passion you have –
We'll move back somewhere to save sometime, or
Continue the moment to charge for war?

Thus, you may lose your life against these men,

And no more shall your glory can withstand!"
But Diomedes, goddess-backed has raised
A scowling voice against his dear comrade:

"Talk no more, I shall summon that fate burst
In front of me than become small, and least,
What style does it differ when I hide skin
Or summon the gods to cover me in?

I dread to fight until my cause is done,
And running away is just for small one!
I'm no small a man, nor the mightiest,
But I shall face whatever I may blest,

I am fresh as ever I have before,
Three or seven times, I have strength a score,
Shall I not leave, until heaven implore
Then I shall listen, when god says no more!

No, I'll meet them, Athena will come sure
And my feet shall not tremble, but endure,
These two men with their horses furious both,
Shall I try to hit one of them! I thought

However, Athena the goddess shall
Craft my ramparts with power from my gall!
And then, both of them, confess on my spearhead,
As you halt the horses tough, on my lead.

Then as fast you halt those horses, take thus
One full hitch around the chariot you must,
And jump on Aineias' horses drive
Away unto Trojan line, but alive.

For I want to kill them by my own hand,
And stampede their fear into the black sand,
And the horses, the finest in the world,
Set forth as fee for Ganymedes lord,

Under Dawn, under Helios, the greatest,
Shall I have them for fee, all their horses!
Ankhises, marshall of Troy, stole these stock,
Without Laomedon's knowledge or a track,

And at his manor he bred them, to full,
Mighty pedigree, and heavenly fall,
From these half a dozen, fillies conceived,
And four were kept, in his manor were reared,

And the two unto Aineias' war car,
If we can get them, honor in our star,
Then, shall we get these horses, for a fame,
And carry us in triumph, with our name!"

The two conferred in this way, as they sworn,
The other pair behind, a full tilt scorn,
And so, they come in range, ready to snatch,
Pandaros called out, a prayer to match:

"O son of Tydeus, heart fearless, whole,
Undauntless in war and heavenly fool!
If my arrowhead could not bring you down,
Let me use the spear, and silence your bone!

That wasted shot on your shoulder has passed,
But unto me a failure encompassed,

God, let me hit you, this bronze spear alas,
So down with your name, and down with your ass!"

Riffled, thumbed, the long spear in the warm air,
Fly like a curse, like a locust wing it dares,
Thus, the point struck into the shield it melts,
Through the cuirass, though not a blood has spilled.

Thus, Pandaros shouts, a great shout indeed,
Thought Diomedes was already killed,
Says he: "O I sing, now you are hit,
What have you wait, standing on those feet?

Not long, I think, for the glory is mine,
Release yourself to pain, it would be fine!
Your lion lust for blood shall need to stop,
Now, you taste my spear, and soon shall you drop!"

Diomedes unshaken by the blow,
Pandaros' spear has not reach skin below,
What he thought is great does not seem profound,
A first rate failure, this person has sound.

Says Diomedes: "What you say, foolish!
I got no hit, and 'gain, your spear has missed!
But I doubt you two will quit, cease the plague,
Until one of you is down with his leg!

Not until Ares' gluttering hands help,
And release your blood off this Trojan kelp,
Then, shall I cease hearing your haughty snare,
When the truth is, your failure is my chair!"

At this, he made his throw, confronting straight,
Guided by Athena, his spear awaits,
To cleave unto Pandaros, kill him bled,
And so it happens that, Pandaros' dead.

The spear is cast pointed unto his nose,
Between his eyes, and shatter his teeth close,
His tongue is severed, bloody red and gross,
Then his breathe flew away sans imposed!

From his car, he toppled down, in the dust,
Clanging his armor, spangled as it was,
Then, his horses shuddered, their master's fall,
And shied the roam about, away his soul.

Life and spirit ebbed, retreating his soul,
The broken man lay still, perishing all.
Though his head uncut, as he wished before,
His head ashamed, by the rash he made to sore!

Aineias on foot, held his spear and shield,
Looks in hatred while the man dragged his yield,
The dead man's body he cursed with his blood,
There, unto Diomedes' hands enshroud.

Like a lion, the man carries his prey,
And shall tear it apart, nearby the bay.
Aineias keep his spear and rounded shield
Before him, and thrusts anyone who filled

The space around; raised a terrible cry.
Diomedes, bent for a stone and fly
Toward Aineias and battered his hip,

A boulder so large no two man can lift.

Into his bone it crashes, thus it shift
What they call the bone-cup, crushing its fit,
Ripping the skin, and fallen on his knees,
Putting his weight on one hand. As to gist,

Night veiled his eyes, dimming in the sun light,
He would have perished on that battle fight
Had Aphrodite, daughter of Zeus, went
To rescue his son, this terrible bent.

As she, her mother, who bore him on earth,
Now has pillowed him, the same as his birth,
But now, under soft shimmers of her robe,
Covers his son against Danaän mob.

Not a spear! Not an arrow would stab him,
And finish his son's life, not in her dream,
Then, from that battle ground, she lifted high,
Aineias heavenward, toward the sky.

Meanwhile, forgetting not Diomedes,
Sthenelos evoked his command – Horses
He brought to a halt, and transferred his stead
Unto Aineias' long-maned charming breed,

Away to the Trojan's reach, he made route
Unto Deipylos' hands, he drove the loot,
For he esteemed this friend more than his peers,
Unto the ships, the horses rest. But fierce

He remount himself back to the chariot,

Checking his wheels, shaking the polished cot,
He drove again with sure-footed horses,
On the dust track unto Diomedes.

Now, Diomedes moved ahead to her,
His furious mood attacks the goddess fair,
He knew the Kyprian goddess is weak,
Not one of those mistresses of war-trick.

Athena, or Enyo, mistress of war,
Has raided cities, and leave them to char,
This goddess, however, battles enfold,
Unlike her sister, war is her stronghold!

Therefore, he made the move, assail her bled,
With a great ruck, unmindful of his head,
Where he leaped high, and aiming his spear fall,
Wounding her hands, trailing against his gall.

Thus, the brazen lancehead, slashed her shawl,
Worked by the Graces themselves, afterall,
Cutting her gentle skin, upon her palm,
The goddess screamed in the terror, uncalm'd.

An immortal fluid, ichor, has flowed,
The blood of immortal gods, blissful glowed,
They who eat no food, or drink tawny wine,
And thereby bloodless, this, immortal sign.

So, as she screamed and flung her child away,
Lord Apollo caught him in his arms sway,
Boring him off safely in a dark cloud,
That no spear would reach him, and kill him proud.

Diomedes, unto Aphrodite,
Cried out to her: "Goddess of beauty,
Give up this war! War and killing, I said,
Is it not enough – and, that I have bade?

To break soft women down, their name derides,
Gentle as the wind of the eastern tides,
Go off, haunting battles, will you, I dare?
Away you flew, otherwise you shudder!

She quit the field, that bloody battle ground,
As Iris helped her through the wind they're bound,
Away in anguish and in fainting pain,
Yet sobbing, the goddess lovely skin gain.

From it, darkness ran on her wound, surround,
Then she came on his brother Ares found,
Resting far on the left, leaning her hand,
Falling on his knees, she begged a demand:

"Brother dear, please let me ride your chariot,
Onwards Olympos should I ride thy cot,
Take me home, dreadfully I was hurt by
A mortal who speared me on the hand, By

Zeus, he'd even fight with him, when he does,
Ah, that Akhaian beast, Diomedes!
Send me home, I might faint from this great pain,
And scatter my ichor, and lost thee insane."

Ares, being moved, lend her his team, at they came
A gold-bangled chariot, everyone's dream,

And into that car, she stepped instantly,
Yet throbbing with pain, she just mind to flee.

Iris is at her side, gathered the reins,
And flicked the horses into much eager veins,
Swiftly the horses moves, they arrive fast,
To steep Olympos, almost one, alas,

The gods dwell herein. Iris, running wind,
Halted and yoked no more the bangled team,
Tossed heavenly fodder on the horses,
Her rescue is done, on a chair she rests.

In Dione's lap, she sank down, throbbed in pain,
Her mother caressed her, in sweet refrain:
"Who did this to you, my darling child, say?
In heaven who could be so brutish gray?

Such rude and wild wound is unfitting grave,
Who committed such an open wrong brave?
No less than bitter, that heavenly flaw,
Less than joy, but dreaded, such act bestowed."

Says Aphrodite, fond of smiling eyes:
"Diomedes wounded me I reprise,
While I tried to save my dear son on war,
And aye, the dearest son of all, my star.

Now, this war has been graver it becomes,
Not only Akhaians against Trojans,
But mortals against their gods, the Argives
Are making war against gods, heaven-lived."

Loveliest of goddess, Dione, she says:
"Patience, dear child of mine, in such distress,
This shall keep you in wisdom, as your aid,
And when you are done, it would heft thy grade.

Many a gods who live on Olympos,
Though powerful, has suffer many loss,
Many have taken hurt from men of war,
And even hurt each other, near or far.

Lo, Ares bound himself bore unto it,
When Otos and Ephialtes had him neat
On a brazen jar for thirteen moons long,
These giant sons of Aloeus had wrong

Laying Ares on that said jar so strong,
Had these war glutton perished with their throng,
Ares won't be free subdued in that curse,
So Eëriboia, their stepmother hearse

To tell Hermes about his suffering,
And that set him free, broke the iron ring.
Second, think of Hera who suffered too,
From the hand of an arrow bower due,

When Amphitryon's mighty son loose a fly
Of a triple-barbed arrow, more than pry,
Unto her right breast struck, woeful she felt,
Unappeasable pain came to her pelt.

Third, Hades, lord of the undergloom, say,
Bore a strong shot from one of Zeus' stout bray,
While there, amidst the dead, undelivered,

From this son of Pylos, received him faired,

In anguish great, he was pierced and stricken,
Went to high Olympos, feeling sicken,
Still with the arrow on his great shoulder,
Paieon healed him though death is not his share.

A poultice is applied, and so healed him,
What recklessness of Hercules, redeemed,
Champion though of labors, must he not shrug
A wicked act against Olympian god.

And now, this man who wounded thee, declare,
He is an idiot, who cannot repair
The dying glow in his candle, numbered,
That happens to anyone who angered

A god, discomfiture at any way,
A curse surrounding his person each day,
This children would not be allowed to sing,
'Papa! Papa!' in all their bright cheering

As he returned after this brutish war,
So let Diomedes breathe sullen hour,
As his pride compose, shall he find a match,
That shall bend his knees, that day shall we watch!

Aigialeia, Adresto's daughter cry,
Starting her night with tears, until eyes dry,
It wakens all the house, missing her man:
Diomedes, noblest of Akhaian."

Dione soothed her, calm her at ease, away

She wiped the ichor on Aphrodite,
She seems fine, already throbbing less than
The first hour she almost faint, with her hand.

But Hera and Athena, looking strict,
Thought of warpish insoluble kick,
That irritates Zeus, even at that time,
Athena the grey-eyed goddess sublime:

"Oh, father, will you be annoyed at me,
When a lesser comment I share with thee?
Aphrodite beguiles women therein
With Akhaia to elope with Trojan,

Whom she adores, or more than that, I say,
Now, fondling some girl, I fear, I dismay,
She scratched her slim hands on a golden pin,
And so she needs to rest from this war 's din!"

He smiled at this, Zeus to pale-god goddess
Says: "Warfare, my child, is not for your best,
Lend yourself to sighs of longing lovers,
And their marriage-bed in fragrance diverse.

Let Athena and Ares deal with war,
And you, my child, be healed, cross not the bar."
These were the discussions in heaven high,
Aphrodite, nothing to do, but sigh.

Meanwhile, brutish Diomedes, on charge,
To Aineias lying in comfort, surge,
Though he knew Apollo sustained him strong,
He feared not even a god, or his throng.

He meant to acquire Aineias' armor,
So three times he tried, a great lethal soar,
But three times Apollo buffeted him,
Throwing him back, less from where he begin.

But nay, Diomedes cease not a fourth,
And with that the Archer god shouts a sort
Of a blood-curling cry: "Look out! Give way!
You poltroon trying to upset my day!

How dare you try a god? Enough of this –
This craze to vie a god, I am not pleased!
Our kind, immortals of the open sky,
Power beyond your life, we cannot die,

And we'll never be like yours, eroding,
An earth-faring man, proudly competing.
Whatever you do, your strength has no cost,
Against me – ah, the Archer am your host!"

That terror made him one or two steps back,
Before Apollo's anger, and its ruck,
Creases his temper against adamant,
And pleat upon this warrior's rudish hand.

So, Apollo caught up Aineias high
On Troy's citadel, on Pergamos shy
Against the war, of blood, and clotting smell,
But in comfort and soft, his fate may dwell.

Apollo's shrine herewith stand, nobly built,
Where Leto and Artemis tended wit,

And honored the man, and heal his bone cup,
While still in veil of night, after the rough.

Meanwhile, Apollo made a figure suit
A magic to double Aeneias foot,
An illusion to fight for him instead,
A phantom armed as he was armed ahead.

Round this phantom, Trojans and Akhaians
Cut one another's chest-protecting stance,
One oxhide after another brought down,
One life after another, wearing down.

Then, Apollo to the wargod, invoke:
"Mankind bane, nuisance of all, in blood soak,
Breacher of walls, ruinous fang and claw,
Why not take this man out this combat now?

This Diomedes, proud as he is, would
Try to cast a fight against Zeus! Be fooled
Not by this man's trickeries, against us,
When he attempted to cut Kypris soft hands,

Then, like a furious lion, came at me.
Take this man off this war, but instantly,
Let him be shrouded in collars of dream,
Until the war is over, so it seems.

Apollo turned away, in a great height,
And to Pergamos he rested a light,
While Ares baleful, marching in with Troy,
Made their way stiffen to kill and destroy!

Thus, Ares marching, like Akamas mien,
A good runner and chief of the Thracians,
To the sons of Trojans, appealing on:
"Princes, thou heir of Priam, Zeus' bone!

How take the suffering when rout they make,
How long would an Akhaian kill and take
Your men's pride, and gallantry, while you fear?
Up to the city gates where all thing's dear?

Lying out there though voiceless in the dust,
One of the Trojans, the best, one of us!
This, Lord Hektor admires, he's Aineias,
Come, let's save him from this brute, routish clash!"

He made them burn in fury, furiously,
And there is none a fear to compass sea,
For Trojans in rage, becomes wilder beasts,
That sweeps the battle ground like full-blown feast.

To Hektor, growled Sarpedon: "What of you,
O prince, Priam's son, your courage gone too?
Defend the city gates, alone but armed,
Will you do this? Can you survive the harm?

March on without allies, without your kin,
Just yourself, without brothers, will you win?
Ah, I have not seen dogs crawling around
A lion, supposed, in this battle ground.

We do the fighting, against Akhaians
We who are allies here, bestrode this chance –
A long journey I suffer, praying verse,

From Lykia to Xanthos' great rivers,

Far away, I left my children their smile,
And a beautiful wife, soft and fragile,
With a house a beggar would like to see,
But what's happening right now, possibly?

Here, I stand before you, fighting forward,
Marching boldly against Akhaians hard,
Though I have no least or great benefit,
And not a booty to carry with it!

And look, you stand like a sheep, amidst us!
Not a word, not a shout, to burn our lust!
Not even a cry, to embrace our ground,
To fight for our own wives! And fight like a hound!

This is helpless, a helpless game indeed,
And your enemies shall feast with their greed,
Inside that city walls, where Priam sits,
That will soon pillage your city, and meets

The shame under your name, without control,
So, this shall be your duty, after all:
Night and day, thou shall press your captains for,
To fight in battleward with full honor!

Tell them, all your foreign allies to keep
His place in the fight, no sooner to sweep
These Akahain dump, rallying in heat,
And shed the bitterness of your defeat!"

This lashing words made Hektor felt the shame,

At these Sarpedon's pounding and the blame,
Down he vaulted at his car, hot engrowled,
Hefting two spears, calling the army howled,

To fight with courage, center and between,
Join the battle steadfast, warring their win,
So the Trojans went rallying about,
Stood off Akhaians, forming as they round.

Imagine: as wind blowing the chaff sway,
On an ancient threshing floor, by the bay,
When men toss up the sheaves, fanning with air,
And yellow-haired Demeter, puffed the lair,

Dividing the chaff from the grain, it piles,
How the sun bleaches whitish the strawpiles,
So white grew the Akhaian army stood,
Figures churned in dust clouds and brazen mood,

By the horses' hooves, chariots melding-in,
Drivers in amalgam stature turned in,
Carrying their hands high, forwarding wall,
Gallantly marching though fatigue install'd.

Coming to the Trojan's aid, Ares hailed,
Covered everywhere in a dusk prevailed,
To such that Apollo's words be obeyed,
To rouse Trojan courage deeply in-veined.

There Apollo's golden sword, surely passed,
Circling around their head, vengeful to slash,
On the other side was Athena's hand,
Guiding, defending her great Danaän!

After a while, Apollo sent him back,
Aineias to battle, restored from shock!
Marshall of the Trojan troops, warrior-lust,
He stands again with his peers, as he must.

The army restored their confidence whole,
Incensed of fury! Mad at the war-fool!
Aineias stands brightly, hot for the war,
Like a new smitten gold from brazen char!

None dare to question him, or ask him some,
None could pause to greet him, their eyes are ram,
Apollo brought a new toil, to meet with,
With Ares and Strife in this war bequeath!

On the midst of them, the two Ajax strong,
With Diomedes, Odysseus along,
These four men bastion, fortress manifold,
Fearless against Trojan power. Behold;

Motionless the clouds above them, and top,
This Zeus made to station, above their grasp,
On high mountaintops with heaven so clear,
The north wind sleeps, and all the winds forbear,

That the clouds remain unmoved, so for long,
Dispels not a shady cloud, masking strong,
In this way, the Danaäns, held their place,
Unstirred from their warcries and foul grimace,

While Agamemnon rode his chariot fast
Haranguing his troops, mighty as he passed.

Says Agamemnon: "Dear friends, be a man!
Valor and pride are clasp between your hands,

When shocks of combat, there's nothing to see
But live one another in victory!
Proud men are saved than men who surrenders,
Who got the praise, and who got it better?

But nay, to a coward, his life untowed,
In the realm of gloom, his name unknown,
And so, move on, be men of pride, ensure,
There is no safety either, in a cure!

But be men, and let history outbright
All doubts of the afterlife, keep your might!
Get afterward the rewards of your praise,
And not anywhere else, but in this place!"

Then, quickness start to affirm his own fiend,
And with his own spear, hit Aineias' friend,
Deikoön, the son of Pergasos,
A spear-fighter, an honored man embossed,

Prompt to join the battle, line a war-lust,
Yet his shield unto Agamemnon's thrust
Has been hit very hard, he can't withstand,
The spearhead drove through his belt, crumpled
down.

And with the clang of his armor, the dark,
Aineias however killed two in hark,
Champions of Danaäns, mighty and high,
It brought a message of fright, to the sky!

These, Ortilokhos and Krethon, brothers,
The sons of Diokles from Pherean heirs,
Descended from the rivers, Phylian land
Called Alpheios, these champions reprimand,

Their early death with Aineias' own hand,
Though they were skillful in all arms demand,
Their heritage gone, their names in the sand.
Fresh in manhood, in a black ship they land

Against the horse country of Illion,
To gain reprisal, vengeance they sworn
With Atreidai, and king Agamemnon,
And Menelaos, shall they fight and worn.

Here Death welcomes their early passing-in,
Imagine two young lions, gathering,
Reared by a lioness, for many months,
From a deep mountain forest, for a haunt,

A twin that prey together, despoiling,
Until one day, shall they be torn, wailing,
Both at once by Aineias' sharp spear claws,
Both of them fell on the ground, undisposed.

Like a pine, tolling lofty, shading wide,
Before an ax, fell husky it complied.
Menelaos pitied the two young men,
Came up with his glittering bronze ascend,

Formidable against, menacing spear,
Indeed, Ares urges him a trap near,

Unto Aineias' hands, his life to bleed,
Had Antilokhos went to join his greed,

Menelaos is conquered in the scene,
So much for Nestor's son, in his coming-in,
Anxious of his captain's fate, siding close,
Shoulder to shoulder with Menelaos!

An agile fighter though he was, decide,
To shun the combat, measuring their wide,
Thus, as he retreat, pulled the corpses twin,
And passed them to the rear, looked deep and keen.

First they killed Pylaimenes, captain
Of the Paphlagonians regiment main,
Menelaos hit him a spear thrust straight,
Piercing him through his collarbone and plate.

Antilokhos knocked his driver, Mydon,
Smashing his elbow from a boulder stone,
In the dust, his ivory inset curled out,
As Atntilokhos leapt on him, gash out

His forehead, a shock covering his soul,
Yet gasping, down he went, a lowly crawl
Toward his car ornate to the sandbank
But his horses move him further the rank,

Into the dust, Antilokhos consigned
To the rear, these horses mighty and fine,
Thus ends this captain's life, pitiful stuff,
Knowing not what would happen on the rough.

Surveying the Akhaians rank and file,
A sudden cry moved his strong Trojan bile,
They held a walled formation-laden arms,
Impelled by Ares and Enyo, to harm

And bring the shameless butchery of war,
Against the foreigners distant far,
Who traveled to seek a lovely lady,
And made war a stunt for one man's fancy.

Thus wielding Ares, his gigantic spear,
In turn leads the prince of Troy without fear,
Backing him up, that not one may cease him,
Diomedes watched all these crazy whim.

Like journey on a sea, a whirlpool rounds,
Or traveler on plain, nowhere to bound,
Helpless to cross the plain or the sea flood,
For in front of him, he sees Ares god!

Thus, Diomedes retreats from the spumes,
Backed away from his company assumes,
Says he: "Friends, at Prince Hektor, marvel we,
There's nothing else to say but lucky he!

What a spearman he is, fighter first rate,
And one of the gods gone, guarding his fate,
Everywhere he goes, covering his skin,
From mortal wounds and gashes, shielding him.

Look, there beside him – Ares battle-wise,
Like a mortal man, candidly disguised!
Protecting Priam's son, what is left us?

Ah, but marvel at him as Hektor does!

Give ground slowly, retreat we must, awhile,
Keep your faces toward the Trojan file,
There is no good pitting ourselves with gods,
It's unseemly to be listed as mad."

Yet the Trojan mightily reaches them,
As he spoke to his assembly proclaim,
Unto Hektor's swift spear, slay him but twains,
Two men of quality, the army pains.

These joy of war – Menesthes, Ankhialos,
Both driving their chariots a single host,
Now, fallen on the dust, a high regret,
Ajax Telemonios pitied their death.

He moved closely, with glittering of spear,
At play with his condolent moods, is clear,
Avenging their death, he overcame one,
The son of Selagos, named Amphion.

This landowner from Paisos, encountered,
His loyalty to Priam is over,
Yet destiny made him Priam's warson,
And unto Priam's son's warlord he stand.

But now, Ajax's spear made it through his belt,
Unto his lower belly the spear melts,
Crunched inside him, and stuck filthy in red,
He fell hard in the dust where he is bred.

Ajax came fast to strip him and his flesh,

His anger's crispy as an apple fresh,
Around him, however, Trojans pending,
Their bright shields and spears such that,
approaching.

He must get his spear stuck in the man dead,
As if the broken man's spirit has fed
On it a curse, he cannot pull it off,
Perchance, with one heel braced on the corpse, off,

He forced away his mainstay against it,
But being best in the spear, nay it slip,
And aye, it stuck unto the dead man's bone,
A brittle fear pounded a deepest tone.

And now, he too must be afraid and shun,
Of Trojans gathering the corpse around,
Brave men pressing him with spears, too many,
His singular bout can't match their plenty.

So the Trojans pushed Ajax back, retired,
A mood shaken, he gathered himself tired.
Everyone must be tired, this toil of war,
That took place in that befamous quarter.

Elsewhere, Fate transports Hercules' great son,
Named Tlepolemos, to meet Sarpedon,
As they reached each other, both kin to Zeus,
Son and Grandson, Tlepolemos caroused:

"Lykian, Sarpedon, famous war consort,
Why so coy, bashful in front of your worth?
You call thyself a fighter? How obvious?

They are liars those who call you from Zeus',

For, you are far inferior as his son,
To those whom Zeus fathered, you are but none,
Among the men of old, your name is lost,
And think, what power have I, but utmost.

My father Hercules, lion-hearted,
His memory rests even among dead,
Remember how he ruin Laomedon
To ransack it with a handful of men?

Ah, six shiploads, and that is all it was,
Beached at Troy, he ran Illion its gash,
And left her desolate, raped and bleak all,
Until this day, it's a threat to appall.

But your nerve and blood, toasting so badly
In the scorches of this old memory!
You and your troops are losing badly, nay,
Retreating badly, for a Lykian prey!

Powerful man, that you are, however,
Shall you fall to me, down the gates enter,
And Death shall you go, you son of a god,
Those liars were telling you from the start!"

Answered Sarpedon: "He did ruin thus
Great Illion – Laoemedon is a trash!
That greedy fool gave him such vicious air,
After the great labors were performed fair.

Yet the refuse to delivery made

Hercules a dragon of ancient shade,
This made him mad, seek what he ought to have.
As for you, this, I say, Death be thy grove.

A bloody death shall you find in this place,
When my spear knocks you out, in sheer disgrace,
You'll give up your glory, of what it was,
And I shall have your name under my hush.

So shall you bless me with your life, I ask,
And to him who drives the horses you must,
Down Hades, of the undergloom, you spent
The rest of your murmurings and foul scent!"

Tlepolemus' ashen spear is raised, yet fast
Was Sarpedon's hands, his long shaft has passed
Almost the instant he raised his hands; mourn,
He hit his enemy right through forlorn,

Squarely in the neck, forcibly thorough,
Tlepolemos went an early night though.
On the same, Tlepolemos point has reached
Hitting his upper leg, jolting through which

The long bones; but once again, Zeus saved him.
Out of the melee, men attended him,
Carried whilst the agony of sound pain,
Encumbered by long bronze spear, very well-trained.

Yet none had time to think how to move out,
The shattering spear, on his leg without,
At least, he may use one leg more, they say,
They did their work, pressed by the battle hey!

Meanwhile, the battered Tlepolemos back
Carried by Akhaians to their bivouac
Thus, rugged Odysseus, in anger burst
Noted what happened, jests the pain it thirsts.

He thought what should be done – track down the
line,
To find Sarpedon, beyond Trojan line?
That son of thunderous Zeus or just take
The life of Lykians in throngs, should he make?

Undecided yet, Athena ushered
To finish the Lykian blood he must bear,
He killed Koiranos, Alastor Khromios,
Noemon, Prytanis, Alkandros, Halios.

And he would have killed more Lykians had not
Hektor's piercing eyes, has cease him the plot,
Under his shimmering helmet, glitters,
With burning bronze, his terror to banters,

Made Sarpedon's heart lifted up, though weak,
Says he: "I beg you, leave me not an irk
To respite here for Danaäns to spoil,
Defend me, O Hektor, this seemless toil.

Then, I must be sure that I bleed away,
My life within the city walls, today,
To see my home, and my country once more,
My wife and my little son, my joyful hour!"

Handsome under his helmet, polished bronze,

Hektor dazzling and impetuous, at once
Passed an order to attack the foes back,
In general slaughter, a fatal crack.

Around Sarpedon, a royal shade, rests,
Under the oak of Zeus, his mourning wrests,
One dear to him, Pelagon, worrying,
Pulled the spearhead on his thigh wound, fainting.

But a cool north wind retrieves his lost breath,
It blew around and fanned him, on his shirt,
Wakened him from the black veil of his swoon,
On Sarpedon's rousing, battle resumes.

Confused were the Argives, yielding over,
They knew Ares attacks them through Hektor,
Even though the ships were not yet routed,
The fear of god's enmity is death!

One by one, Hektor slew these fighting men,
First is Teuthras, Orestes the horseman,
Breaker of horses and a spear-thrower,
Trekhos the Aitolian, first-rate soldier.

Then, Oinomaos, and Helenos
Oinopides, and Oresbios,
Whose brass breast late glitters like demi-ghast,
He once live at Hyle, on lake Kephisos!

Fond of his wealth, his comrades attended,
Unto Boiotians fertile plain, he laired.
Now, these great men, joy of the Argives, were dead,
A vital loss to the army ahead.

Now, Hera seeing how frightened, they flee,
Perish the Argives wanton of the sea,
Appealed to Athena, in ire she says:
"What a dismal event has just took place!

It seems that our words to Menelaos
Is a fraud! Is this the wander I choose?
That he should not, no, in his home revive,
Before preying Illion by Argive!

It would be likely some foolishness say
From a god, when our promise comes to clay,
Should we permit Ares this lunacy,
That sinister fool against our treaty!

Come, let's put our minds together, and see,
How would we overwhelm this Trojan spree?"
Grey-eyed Athena to Hera attests,
Listened on her words with joy and prudence.

So Hera, daughter of Kronos, she was,
Harnessed the team, all golden fringes must,
On her chariot held, Hebe fittingly,
From left and right, its brazen wheels lorry,

Eight shinbones spokes around an axle-tree,
It was made of iron, supremacy,
Yet all aurum her felloes are, unworn,
Tire of bronze, a marvel to the unborn!

Lo, the hubs are silver, hinted in gold,
Woven together, in a double fold,

And her car, a silver pole leans forward,
A grandiose chariot from the godly ward!

Hebe fitted the tip, with golden yoke,
And added collars, all of soft gold stroke,
Hungry Hera for a strike in the war,
Her sure-footed horses, terrible to scar!

Athena, with the same mind, as to her,
Casts off and dropped her robe, as it appear,
Yet hiding underneath was Zeus' storm-shirt,
A stronghold of thunder and storm-cloud birth,

With breast armor and hint to grieve the war,
Athena stole thus from the storm-master.
She hung the stormcloud shield, with braided veil,
Ominous from her shoulder, such an ail.

Around it hung in a garland, unleashed
Rout in a figure, and its clout revealed,
The same with Enmity, of Force, and Chase,
Chills the blood, in the midst of Fear, embraced.

The Gorgon's head, a reptilian, of old,
Portent of the stormking, this monster hold,
Thus, Athena four times golden-crested,
Double-ridged her helmet, hundred times best!

She took a great shaft on her hand, heavy,
Yet this child of Power can use; Misty
Were the hours, the clouds aloof in her name,
Just to break the fright and the men of shame.

Then, Hera, at the crack of her whip, awed,
The horses to show-off t heir regal road,
The gates of heaven opened widely then,
Swung the chariot its rumbling hinges send!

The gate of Hours keep the affairs she lead,
For it is charge with the storm clouds ahead,
The opening and closing, and passing,
Of gods and their affairs, and safekeeping.

Thus, along the pass, Hera encountered
The son of Kronos who sat in the center,
Apart from all other gods, reigning pleased,
She addressed the all-highest god, in this:

"O mighty Zeus, are you not ill enough,
Unto Ares' brutal acts and his rough?
How great and how grave the Akahaians flee?
A great body he destroyed wantonly!

He grieved unfairly, while Kypris fair
And Apollo, mighty god of warfare,
Take their pleasure of this battle I share,
We have treated unfairly this affair.

Now urging the dunce, who knows not fairly,
Shall we observe what is true decency!
Might Zeus, you cannot annoy this day,
While I chastise and chase him my own way!"

Then, Zeus who gathers cloud replied to her:
"O Hera of my heart, Hope of Soldier!
Athena, you are the one matching him.

You have wondrous way grieving his whim."

At this permission, Hera cracked her whip,
Racing between heaven and earth, the grip
Of her horses faster than sound must have flown,
In the dark distance between them is torn.

As a wine-dark sea, the distance dimming,
The horses bound to earth, fast and neighing,
In the upper air, upon Trojan plain,
The two rivers run with blood in its vein –

Skamander flowing, to confluence with
Simoeis, she let her horses complete
Their graze within the ambrosial grass grow,
Soft beyond pasture, this goddess endow.

Then, at height, the goddesses went a-floor,
In a straight line, gliding like a sparrow,
Approached these mighty fairness defending
Their Argives spearmen like sweet caressing.

They arrived where great Diomedes soar,
Giving growls like a lion or a boar,
Here, their greatest men fought, like carnivores,
No feeble their victims, mangled of course.

Now, Hera made her stand, a cry invoked,
Like unto Stentor's figure, trumpet woke!
Whose lungs has the power of fifty brass,
A shout so powerful and loud he has!

Says she: "Shame, Argives! Shame, thy cowardice!

You are but good only on parodies!
You stand like mighty warriors, less than that,
Your looks deceives many but us, cannot.

While Prince Akhilleus roam, Trojans hide,
Never would their faces appear on sight,
For the fear of his mighty name, they shun,
Respecting greatly this mighty of man!

But look, right now, where have they gone? They fight
Far from the city gates, our foes delight!
And near our ships, they shall burn with their fire,
How coward are you – this moment of dire!"

Thus, the shout angered the Argives aloof,
The fury once again has reached their roof!
Meanwhile Athena hastened the great stout
Diomedes, cooling off some fresh clot.

By his car, resting for a while, to cool,
Hence Pandaros' arrow made him a fool,
With sweat under his strap, blood flowing still,
Spent and drenched his strength, yet vital his will.

His shield encumbered, weary of the day,
He slipped the strap off, wiped his blood away,
The goddess put her hand, in this burden,
And the yoke is eased, the goddess ascends:

"Ah yes, a far cry have I heard, bellows.
Sweet father's voice, robust as it mellows,
Thy father's a small man, but a fighter,

Once I forbade him war, even a snare

To trap someone to quarrel over with,
But as a born fighter, I cannot cease.
As a messenger then, your father is,
To Thebes, detached from Akhaian peace,

Amidst Kadmeians in their multitude,
He dine with them in a pure solitude,
Bidden as he was a guest of honor,
And combative in nature and valor,

He challenged the young Kadmeians to brawl,
And he stayed atop, nothing to trouble,
Thus, pinning them all, took his part so well,
And in heaven I've mentioned it as well.

But look at you now, I stand here with you,
By heaven's protection, I care for you!
And so, I tell you to fight, for you should,
Neither you are sluggish, for you are rude,

Nor battle-weary from the cold-blood flow,
Nor hollow-hearted, for your eyes still glow,
Somehow, with fear: but you are not, I say,
Tydeus Oineides son, obey!"

Proud Diomedes answered her, says he:
"O daughter of Zeus, I know you well, see
The stormcloud on your greyish eyes and head!
With all respect, I must explain ahead,

No fear abounds me, no weariness too,

I simply bear in mind your knack undue,
That command to stay behind, and fight not
Any higher being, immortal god,

That is, unless Aphrodite would come,
Should I wound her, for weak is her gram,
So as you commanded me, stay behind,
I ordered the army to ground and mind

That Ares is fighting against our men,
Though shoulder to shoulder here, I pretend,
That the fight should be noiseless as my mind,
Though my heart says I must in fury, find.

Says Athena: "Diomedes, my dear,
Dear to my heart – stand up, focus your spear,
What I have said before, I excused you,
You must not belittle thyself undue,

You must fight against Ares, for I am
With you! Now, call on your team, with a drum,
And onward to Ares, challenge his war,
Hit him hand-in-hand, hit him scar-to-scar!

Defer this war-lust god, maniac of blood,
He is evil-natured, two-faced and mad,
Not one hour ago, I heard him grunt, say,
His words to Hera to fight in your pray,

On the Argives side, that is. But right now,
He forgets everything, and joins the show
Where he foght for the Trojans awfully,
And damaged the Argives tremendously!"

Diomedes, even as she spoke, went
To elbow Sthenelos, and threw the lent,
But he gave a quick hand-up, from the ground,
While she herself summon the great war-crowd.

Impetuous of war, hasty to fall,
Unto Trojan victors, her mind is gall,
At her step the oaken axle groaned loud,
Having to load a hero and a god.

Then, unto her whip, the horses she drove,
Straight to Ares flew, the champion above,
A god and a hero together soared
To seek Ares' silence for his discord.

This brute, as he was, despoiling up mess,
One, a giant from the Aitolian's best,
This Periphas, scion of Okhesios,
The blood-stained god drowned the enormous host.

Now, Athena, unseen by Ares' eyes,
Put on the helmet of Hades, chastise,
But Ares saw Diomedes, whirling,
Left Periphas where it fell, unhiding,

Straight the ruffian god for Diomedes,
At their close, the wargod aims at his chest,
And unto the horses, rifled his spear
Over the yoke and reins, murderous sneer!

But, grey-eyed Athena, with one hand caught,
And deflected the force his brother wrought,

So sending the car and the horses safe,
Bounding harmless, the golden chariot saved.

Now, the heat is on, Diomedes drear
All his weight behind his bronze-headed spear,
Then Athena rammed it toward the waist,
On his belt, toward his flesh! Then haste

Covered mighty Ares growl, pulled again
The spear – so shout he like ten thousand men
In long battalion line, toward heaven,
Terrible to hear, as thunder descend.

A pang of fear ran through the hearts of all,
Below the earth, both armies helpless soul,
Deafened by such a loud roar in the sky,
Insatiable Ares, voracious cry!

A vapor, blackish in a thunderhead,
Rides aloft on storm wind brewing its stead,
As he rose heavenward, amidst the cloud,
Yet he looked up Diomedes astound.

High on Olympos, crag of immortals,
He came by resting unto Zeus' great halls,
Aching yet embarrassed, he showed his wound,
And querulously addressed him: "I would,

O Father Zeus, this matter be accept?
To take insubordination she present?
What frightful things we bear 'gainst another
Doing good things to men, that, I would dare!

And I must say, all these things, under you
Yet you conceived a daughter shameful true,
Without prudence, a destroyer, and vile,
Given to violence, and all things guile!

We, other gods, obey you, as you please,
Submissive indeed are we, none the least,
While she goes unreproved, never a word,
A gesture so wise should come from you, Lord.

O that insolent daughter, I address,
She is the one who urged Diomedes,
First, he closed with Kypris, and cut her palm,
And now, he hurled against, turned me damn.

It was my speed that got me off, or I
Should summon the dead to catch me and die?
That foul dead, undone by further strokes worst,
Then I shall be a noiseless god, foremost!"

But Zeus who masses cloud, frowned at him, says:
"Come not, whining here, I was so displaced
Of your two-faced brutishness, thug ruffian,
Most hateful to me of all Olympian!

Combat and brawling are styles and passion,
These are the elements, your intention,
This beastly, incurable truculence
Comes from your mother, goddess Hera; hence,

Keeping her under my command, I woe,
Barely in my power your mother grow,
Still, I will not have you suffer longer,

After all, my child, I am your father.

Your mother bore you as a son to me,
If you are born to another, you'll see,
Your place would be far below the heaven,
That, being so, for you're born insolent!"

So come Paieon to attend to his wound,
Sprinkled anodyne, thus it would heal soon,
So he started to treat and heal Ares,
Who was not born for death,   He rests

In comfort of the Olympian chamber,
Delivered unto him, the divine care,
As wild fig sap, when dripped in liquid milk
Clots as fast as it is, so his wound shrink.

Then Hebe bathed him, and dress him afresh,
And down he sat beside his father's mesh,
Glowing again in splendor, Ares hailed,
As all the other gods, this great hall mailed.

As soon as Zeus is home they're called to tire,
Argive Hera the queen made it no ire,
Boiotian Athena made Ares quit,
He who made the bane of mankind a feat.*

ABOUT THE AUTHOR

ZALDY C. DE LEON JR.

The author is a graduate of bachelors degree in education and theology, masters of arts in religious education and divinity, and doctorate degree in christian education, theology. He also received honorary degrees in peace, humanities, leadership, theology, and applied cosmic anthropology from Brazil, Sweden, Switzerland, Serbia, India, Haiti, the Caribbean, and other parts of the world for his contribution in the said fields.

www.ingramcontent.com/pod-product-compliance
Lightning Source LLC
Chambersburg PA
CBHW050508160726
48003CB00001B/211